C000026211

LESSONS FROM HISTORY

LESSONS FROM HISTORY

HIDDEN HEROES AND VILLAINS FROM THE PAST AND WHAT WE CAN LEARN FROM THEM

ALEX DEANE

Biteback Publishing

First published in Great Britain in 2021 by
Biteback Publishing Ltd, London
Copyright © Alex Deane 2021

ISBN 978-1-78590-710-4

10 9 8 7 6 5 4 3 2 1

A CIP catalogue record for this book is available from the British Library.

Set in Adobe Caslon Pro and Trade Gothic

Printed and bound in Great Britain by
CPI Group (UK) Ltd, Croydon CR0 4YY

For my late father, Paul Deane.

CONTENTS

INTRODUCTION

This collection began life as a series of stories told on Twitter, where my handle is @ajcdeane, under the hashtag #deanehistory. The tales told there are still available, along with many interesting digressions and responses from hundreds of people who love history as much as I do. However, freed from the strictures of the Twitter format, the stories that reappear here have been extended and elaborated on, and many other stories appearing here were not posted online.

I began telling the stories as a distraction for myself during the coronavirus lockdown, as my father was dying. Caring for him at home with my family, I was surrounded by his great collection of works of history, which reflected his wide-ranging and random interests that are reflected here.

In his last days, he took great interest in the progress of this book, and, though inadequate as a tribute, it is dedicated to his memory.

Alex Deane
Bury St Edmunds
August 2021

CHAPTER 1

JEAN-BAPTISTE BERNADOTTE

Jean-Baptiste Bernadotte joined the French Army when his ambitions of following his father into the law were stymied by his father's death. He was a brilliant soldier and gained rapid advancement.

He married a woman who had previously been engaged to Napoleon and was the Emperor's older brother's wife's sister; those Bonapartes liked to keep things tight. (Hey, Joseph, be King of Naples! No, be King of Spain!)

In the War of the Fourth Coalition,* the Prussians under Blücher were taking a beating at the hands of the French. Blücher, one of the most feted and decorated German / Prussian officers of all time, was nicknamed Marshall Forward by his men in honour of his aggressive fondness for advancing. Such tendencies were not in evidence in this encounter. In 1806, at the Battle of Lübeck,†

---

* The Coalitions concerned France and whoever was on board for a fight against Napoleon at a given time. There were seven in all, the last of course ending with Waterloo and exile. It's a pretty complimentary numbering system when one thinks about it: France against all comers – that's that one done; now, who's next?

† Lübeck is a beautiful Hanseatic port. Beginning with north German coastal towns in the late twelfth century, the Hanseatic League came to dominate Baltic maritime trade for three centuries along the coasts of northern Europe and was a strong, enduring link between British ports and their northern continental counterparts. It was both a commercial and a defensive confederation of merchant guilds and towns in northern and eastern Europe, where its history is remembered far more than in the UK, where – as so often – we have largely forgotten the ties of the past.

Bernadotte and co. caught Blücher's retreating army and marmalised them.

Reflecting the 'everyone against the French' trend of the era, there were some Swedes fighting at Lübeck alongside the Prussians. Bernadotte captured them and treated them courteously and well – he also tried in vain to treat Lübeck well, just as his men sacked it.

Having more pressing things to do than keep a clutch of Scandinavians captive, Bernadotte released them soon after the battle. The Swedes headed home to a problem. The King was heirless and going senile. Who should be the new King? Hey, how about that nice Frenchman who was so decent to us at the Battle of Lübeck? Plus, he's close to the Emperor; that can't hurt…

Thus, a Frenchman came to be ushered onto the throne of Sweden, giving us the House of Bernadotte, which reigns to this day.

What's the lesson we might take from this story? When you have got the whip hand, sometimes it pays to be nice. People remember it. This is a lesson I believe to be applicable beyond one's behaviour to defeated nineteenth-century Swedish minor nobility.

Anyway, he was Crown Prince for a while, but as the King was well and truly gone by the time of his appointment in 1810, Bernadotte was running things PDQ. What did the newly Swedish Crown Prince do? Why, he took his new country to war. Against France. What can one say? The man had elan.

CHAPTER 2

LORD HAW-HAW'S CAPTURE

Lord Haw-Haw, real name William Joyce, was the voice of the Nazis on air during the Second World War and was, of course, the last person executed for treason in the UK – so far, so well known.

Less well known is the fact that after the war he was captured near Germany's border with Denmark, in woodland outside Flensburg, the last capital of the Third Reich, by a British intelligence unit who recognised him by his distinctive accent. Specifically, he was caught by an officer called Geoffrey Perry (born Horst Pinschewer), a Jewish German who'd fled the Nazis and signed up with us Brits.

Perfect, yes? But it gets better.

Believing (he claimed) that Haw-Haw was going for a gun, said Jewish intelligence officer shot him. In the arse. *Through* the arse, in fact. Four wounds: entry and exit through both buttocks.

These are *not* life-threatening injuries, but they *are* deeply humiliating and painful.

I suggest that takes a high level of accuracy.

* * *

'I'm not a conspiracy theorist, but...'

3

The author Nigel Farndale has established that Joyce had properly evidenced and not-fantasist pre-war connections to the British secret service MI5. At his trial at the Old Bailey, he did not mention this or give evidence at all, or have his barrister put this to anyone, despite the fact that it might have saved him from the gallows. It is difficult to think of an explanation for this, especially given the inevitable consequences of his silence, other than the possibility that he had made a bargain with those prosecuting him not to raise it – avoiding the considerable embarrassment to the British state that it would cause – in return for them not prosecuting his wife, who was a rabid pro-Nazi just as guilty of collaboration as he was. She went scot-free – or free enough, at least, to live until 1972, drinking herself to death.

Even knowing what it would mean for his future if he were to keep silent about his past, Joyce, I think, struck a deal: his life for hers.

CHAPTER 3

JOHN THE BLIND

John of Bohemia, the son of the Holy Roman Emperor, was also known as John the Blind. He was – and I may have given this away – visually impaired.

He didn't let this condition (which developed in his late thirties, from ophthalmia – do take your eyedrops if you get conjunctivitis) get in the way of his empire building and army leading, and as was the way at the time, in the end all roads led to having a scrap with the English. At Crécy in 1346.

It is an understatement to say that it was a bad day for the French and their allies. England's forces, under Edward III and his son the Black Prince, demonstrated the superiority of the longbow in a comprehensive defeat of a much larger force. By the way, after Crécy the English successfully besieged Calais, resulting in the Pale of Calais; territory in northern France being held by England for over two centuries, with representative MPs sitting in our Parliament and so forth; and some seriously good art from Rodin.

Anyway – though he had by this point been blind for a decade, John of Bohemia commanded the advance guard of King Philip VI of France at Crécy.* On hearing that

---

* Philip and Edward disputed the succession to the French throne after the death of Charles IV. Our Edward was Charles's nephew; Philip was Charles's cousin. Their dispute began the Hundred Years War.

the battle went against them, John ordered two of his noblemen to tie his mount between them and ride him into battle so he could fight. This exceptional bravery was admired by all Englishmen who saw it.

I mean, we killed him, obviously. But we were seriously impressed.

Such was the Black Prince's admiration for John that, one version of the story goes, he took John's symbol for his own. Thus, nigh on 700 years later, three ostrich feathers are the symbol of the Prince of Wales to this day.

The next time you see an old 2 pence piece or a Welsh rugby top, you'll think of John the Blind.

CHAPTER 4

PAYNE BEST AND THE VENLO INCIDENT

We're heading back to the Second World War in this story, but whilst in Lord Haw-Haw's case we looked at the very end, this is the very beginning.

Captain Sigismund Payne Best was a monocle-sporting British intelligence officer who served in both world wars. Based in the Netherlands between the wars, he ran our spy network in Holland and was drawn into a trap by the Nazis, who dangled officers supposedly representing those in Germany who were interested in removing or assassinating Hitler. But were really, er, Nazis.

A series of meetings took place between Best and his team and the fake plotters. The aim was to humiliate the Brits, to paint us as manipulating / abusing Dutch neutrality and to provide a pretext for saying the Dutch were violating their own said neutrality – claims that were not entirely without merit.

As with much good subterfuge, the Nazis played hard to get, making Best and co. fret that they didn't believe he was really an intelligence agent. We obligingly played some agreed codewords over the BBC to assure them he was.

A series of meetings took place, the location nudging closer to the German border each time – until finally they agreed to meet at Café Backus just outside Venlo, right on the Dutch / German border. With Best was Richard Stevens, a major under official diplomatic cover at our embassy in The Hague. Mixing non-official and official cover is a spook no-no, as *Mission: Impossible* fans will know.

Actually, the whole of our set-up in The Hague was a bit daft. The British 'passport office' (of spooks) was massive, even though it served a country for which Brits didn't need visas. Maybe they were anticipating border crossing ham sandwich snatching.[*]

Also with our spies were two Dutchmen: Dirk Klop, an intelligence officer pretending to be British, and Jan Lemmens, who did some driving for Best.

At this last meeting, on 9 November 1939, on Himmler's orders the SS ambushed and (literally) dragged the men over the border a few feet away. They shot and killed the brave Klop (who I *think* was the first Dutch casualty of the war). They released Lemmens in 1940. The Brits, they kept.

They weren't the first British prisoners of war – Larry Slattery (an Irishman) was shot down over Wilhelmshaven the day after war was declared – but they were amongst the first, and they served the whole war as POWs. In Best's case, he was kept mostly in Sachsenhausen, then in Buchenwald and then in Dachau. Best's memoir is mostly about his warders and his observations of German society. A bit like a Teddy Kennedy book that falls open to

---

[*]   A lorry driver's ham sandwich was seized by the Dutch authorities in the heady days after the end of the Brexit transition period.

Chappaquiddick but deals with it in a page, Best's memoir pretty much skips over the Venlo Incident that made him famous. Given the blunders involved, perhaps that's understandable. But it's a fascinating read about the peculiarities and mundanities of life as a prisoner. The everyday accommodations reached with people with whom relationships are formed, even despite their membership of objectively the worst organisation in human history and so on.

An observation he makes that stayed with me: the Germans had unbelievable stoicism and endurance when it came to the increasingly frequent and increasingly heavy Allied bombing raids, taking to cellars etc. throughout – but they were utterly terrified of the lone fighter appearing from nowhere to strafe streets.

Another character, Stevens – a former policeman in Imperial India and a well-credentialed man – was a fellow prisoner alongside Best who spoke fluent Arabic, German, Greek, Hindi, Russian and Malay. But he didn't speak common sense. Unbelievably, he was carrying an uncoded list of the British agents across Europe in his pocket when he was captured.

The Venlo episode is pretty much forgotten now, but it was quite consequential. First, Germany used it as the pretext for the invasion of the neutral Netherlands. Second, the British network on the Continent was pretty much rolled up at the end of 1939 and the start of 1940, with appalling consequences for the brave people involved, and Stevens's list is a large part of the reason for that. Appalled by the episode, Churchill as PM created the Special Operations Executive.

Best was plainly brave, but he can hardly be said to have had 'a good war'. Suckered into a trap, ingloriously captured, he spent the war moaning about camp dentistry and the inadequacy of Red Cross deliveries, seemingly blind to the suffering of many prisoners, especially Jewish. As one of the first prisoners of war, before the privations of mass captivity really set in (and as something of a 'celebrity' prisoner), incongruously he had huge amounts of stuff delivered to him from his home – including various wardrobes and their contents and so forth. He talks about that and the challenges of storage at bizarre length in his memoirs. (If you're after a British author who writes well about being a prisoner of war kept in the concentration camps, Colin Rushton's *Spectator in Hell* about his time in Auschwitz is utterly haunting.)

A passing reference made to the Venlo Incident in Malcolm Muggeridge's memoirs (which are also recommended) had me down the history wormhole online, buying Best's book and ultimately visiting Café Backus – which is still there – in 2017, which is why as one of the leading political consultants of our age with my finger truly on the pulse of current events, I was in, er, remote south Holland when the UK snap election that year was called by Theresa May.

What's the lesson we might take from this (apart from being more on top of when elections are going to happen if you work in politics)? I think that it's to note the smart lure. Not the snatch at the border – that had all the sub-tlety of Michael Bay's *Pearl Harbor*. I mean the long con run by the Germans to get the British agents there – like all good slow-played con tricks, it made the victims *want* to go further.

Best writes well and comes across as palpably decent. But in our darkest hour, we entrusted our European spy network to a man who today would turn up at a far-flung airport, shocked – shocked! – to find that the charming online bride-to-be to whom he'd sent all that money wasn't there to meet him.

CHAPTER 5

PLATAEA

This is a happy story, and then a sad one.

In the 520s BC, the little city state of Plataea asked Sparta for an alliance, as they feared the Thebans. Mischievously, Sparta told them to ally with Athens, enemy of Thebes; they were angry when that alliance was actually agreed. Careful what you joke about, Spartans.

Quite separately, King Darius of Persia's army marched westwards. Their primary beef was with Athens, a city Darius had sworn to burn to the ground, but it was plainly bad news for all Greeks. Led by the great General Miltiades, the Athenians marched to face the Persians – at Marathon in 490 BC. The Athenians sent for help. (Pheidippides or Philippides, deliverer of long-distance messages, ran through the fennel fields of the region for which the town was named; marathon means 'fennel' in Ancient Greek.)

But no help came. Not even from martial Sparta, who said they were busy observing a festival and therefore couldn't possibly march until the next full moon, which would be far too late; thanks, Sparta. Camped alone and frightened on the plain the night before battle, Athenian sentinels spied dust clouds in the distance and feared a second Persian Army was descending upon them.

But it was the Plataeans. In Athens' hour of need, the plucky Plataeans had come '*panstratiá*' – drop everything; send everyone. All 1,000 of them. Their contribution to Athens's might may have been small, but for Athens to no longer stand alone against this great enemy meant everything. Athenians and Plataeans fought bravely alongside one another as equals that day. They faced a far stronger force. But the battle was won.

Later on, the Plataeans were attacked by the Thebans and besieged by the Spartans in the Peloponnesian War. They fought for two years, and their small numbers were diminished yet further when they sent a force to break through the besiegers to seek help from Athens. Those who joined that enterprise were thought to have volunteered for a suicide mission, but they made it to their allies – only to find that the Athenians declined to come to the aid of the Plataeans, fearing a broader conflict that might result.

After a long, hard winter, starved of supplies and unrelieved by the Athenians, the Plataeans surrendered on the basis that they would be treated fairly.

Instead, the Spartans conducted 'a trial' – each man was asked if he had helped the Spartans and their allies in the war. Why, the very point of Plataea's position was that they were allied – as Sparta knew better than anyone! – to Athens. Thus, each man answered the question, 'No' – and was executed. One by one. Imagine the stoicism, the bravery, to be the 200th man in the queue, waiting your turn to deliver your honourable and honest answer before the sword.

Except for those few who had escaped the siege in the forlorn breakout to Athens, living on as the stateless sons of a vanished city, Plataea's men were dead. Their women and children were sold into slavery. The city was razed to the ground. The land was given to the Thebans.

What's the lesson to be drawn from the sad fate of the Plataeans? I suppose it's this: all friends are great when *they* need *you*. Only some friends are great when *you* need *them*. This episode gives us one of the driest and most brutal lines in history, from Thucydides: 'Such was the end of Plataea, in the ninety-third year of her alliance with Athens.'

CHAPTER 6

THE GEORGIAN UPRISING

Beer brought me to this one.

The Dutch island of Texel produces some very fine beer. It was also the site of one of the last, and most unusual, battles of the Second World War in Europe. (I'm hardly the first Englishman to be interested in the chain of Frisian Islands to which Texel belongs; it's the setting of Germany's then fictitious but deliberately portentous invasion plans in Erskin Childers's brilliant pre-First World War novel *The Riddle of the Sands*.) The Wehrmacht had a 'Georgian Legion'. Some were Georgians who had fled westwards after the Soviet invasion of their (beautiful) country and hated the Soviets. Rather more were captured Georgian soldiers.

Those soldiers were given a choice by the Germans: go to the camps as prisoners, or fight with us (with the rations and perks of being soldiers) as a unit against the Russians. Given the conditions in the camps, what would you have chosen?

The Queen Tamar* battalion of the Georgian Legion had been sent to Texel as part of the Nazi 'Atlantic Wall'

---

* That the unit into which these soldiers were forced to serve was crassly named after the foremost monarch of proud Georgia's golden age must have made their servitude all the more bitter. (Tamar the Great was the first woman to rule Georgia, 1184–1213. No relation to the river that marks the border between Devon and Cornwall.)

– the enormous fortification of German-held Europe against Allied invasion. But, as the backstory implies, their hearts weren't in it.

Told they would be moved from Texel to face Allied advances on the Continent, the Georgians had other ideas. Overnight, on 5–6 April 1945, in the Georgian Uprising against their Nazi masters (with gallant help from Dutch resistance), they took over much of the island. It took the Germans over a *month* to take back the island. Combat was fierce. When battle proper had ceased, irregular resistance continued, with Dutch families hiding Georgians when they could.

The Dutch sometimes get a hard time when the topic of wartime resistance is discussed, so this concealment of foreign fighters far from home in their ditches, dykes and houses pleases all the more. Amazingly, hundreds of Georgians survived in hiding amongst the Texel people until after the war – at which point the Allies promptly turned them over to the Soviets, under the agreements made by the great powers at Yalta. Whilst not as bad as later claimed by some, or as bad as the fates of others who were returned to Russia after the war – that is, they weren't all summarily slaughtered or put into camps – their fate was hardly a happy one.

Still, never ones to miss a propaganda trick, the Soviets turned the Georgian Uprising into a tale of Soviet heroes, complete with annual ceremonial visits to Texel from their ambassador to Holland until the USSR fell and a feature film that simply pretended the rebels had been POWs, not Wehrmacht fighters.

It is not a straightforward story. Some amongst the Georgians will have been willing fighters for Germany. Some amongst the Germans will have been unwilling conscripts, knifed to death in their sleep by the Georgians they had thought to be their allies. But the Georgians were on the right side of history. And from those coerced to serve by the threat of the camps to those who served because their homeland had suffered under the Soviets, their lives had been dictated by forces beyond their control.

Thus was the fate of so many vassal states and their subjects throughout history, and that is what prompted me to think of this after the Plataea episode. That and the fact that beer has a strong influence on the places I read up on.

What's the lesson from this story? Perhaps it's that if you forced somebody into something in the first place, then you can hardly expect them to cleave to the terms and conditions throughout...

Lest this all sounds too gloomy, be assured it's the *second* thought I have when ordering Texels beer in an Amsterdam bar* – the first being quiet admiration for the fact that whilst the brewery has a truly enormous output, the tiny island only exports half of it.

---

* Bars are a sort of public socialising and drinking space, used widely by people in the time before coronavirus.

CHAPTER 7

LEGIONNAIRES ON THE TARMAC

Simon Murray is a magnificent lunatic who told his girl-friend that if she didn't agree to marry him, he would join the French Foreign Legion. She didn't, and he did.[*]

Later recorded in one of the most compelling military memoirs of our time (*Legionnaire*), Murray fought in the Algerian war of independence. His memoirs are – and this is the largest #deanehistory understatement so far – not politically correct.

There are many, many human-interest stories in his memoirs; some are of bravery; others lavatorial; others grim as can be. Suffice it to say he found himself amongst some of the toughest sorts on earth and had to muck in accordingly. I'll choose one bigger-picture story to share.

In 1961, things were touch and go for de Gaulle. 'The Generals' – retired army leaders and a group of old-school French colonialists around them – opposed the French government's efforts to negotiate a peace with the anti-colonialists. A coup was very possible.

The legion's position was key. The long-threatened day of action came: Murray's comrades seized Algiers. He and his unit drove in some pomp to the airport, cheered on

---

[*]   She did later.

their way by hundreds of flag-waving *pieds-noirs* (French colonialists in Algeria).

Marines loyal to de Gaulle protected the airport. But not for long. The legionnaires were more numerous and, one dare venture, rather tougher. This is the sharp end of a coup: army unit against army unit. Soon, the legion held the airport too.

Murray and co. slept in the hangar overnight, ready for a flight to Paris and the removal of de Gaulle the next day. But the energy of the coup petered out as de Gaulle openly appealed for support on the airwaves (or rather, given it was de Gaulle, he *ordered* it), and the people of France rallied to their President.*

The plotters were rounded up; the legion was stood down. Murray and his unit drove back through silent, deserted streets, every window barred, every back turned to them. The legendary 1st Legion Parachute Regiment was disbanded. The legion builds their own barracks; overnight, they blew up their own. Those legionnaires sent to other units marched out singing – truly, life knows better images than art – '*Je ne regrette rien*.'

Murray did his full five-year turn in the Foreign Legion. Afterwards, he married the girl, forged a remarkably successful business career (on the board of many businesses you know), became the oldest man (at sixty-three) to reach

---

* Malcolm Muggeridge was in Paris after the war and attended a service of thanksgiving at Notre Dame. A car backfired outside the church and, with the communal instinct of people who had endured years of war, the entire congregation dived for the floor – except, Muggeridge saw as he looked up from the deck, the person at whom someone might most plausibly have been shooting: de Gaulle, the tallest man there, stood tall throughout.

the South Pole unsupported, is a CBE and a Chevalier de la Légion d'Honneur.

He lives in Hong Kong, is now eighty-one and is probably wrestling alligators with an arm tied behind his back as I type.

CHAPTER 8

THE AROOSTOOK WAR

Maine's Aroostook County (or simply 'The County' to those in Maine) is massive. It is the largest county east of the Mississippi and it's bigger than three US states. But it could have been bigger.

The Treaty of Paris brought the American Revolutionary War to a close in 1783, but it didn't define the border between the USA and British North America precisely. This mattered in Maine (which was not yet a state).

In the war of 1812, which went rather well for the UK, much of Maine was occupied by the British. When the war was over, attempts to define the border more precisely were again unsuccessful.

After Maine became a state in 1820, the issue reared its head again. King William of the Netherlands was asked to arbitrate. Reconciling the treaties with the maps was so hard that William gave up and proposed a compromise between the parties. Under William's terms, Britain would get 4,119 square miles of territory and the USA would receive 7,908 square miles. Britain accepted the compromise; the USA did not.

Tensions mounted. Forces were amassed. The 'Aroostook War' commenced. Whilst the 'war' had no casualties, two militiamen were, in the most Canadian thing ever, injured by black bears. In truth, neither side really wanted conflict.

Cue the Webster–Ashburton Treaty, which settled the border as we have it today. The USA got 7,015 square miles; the British got 5,012 miles. Had the Americans simply accepted William's compromise, America would be circa 900 square miles larger today.

This, by the way, still didn't resolve things entirely. The USA and Canada continue to be at odds over Machias Seal Island (population: zero, bar lighthouse keepers) and North Rock (population: zero). The view, or views, of black bears on these outstanding issues remain unknown.

Amusingly, in the course of the Webster–Ashburton business, the British had a map that suggested support for the American case and the Americans had a map that suggested support for the British case. Naturally, neither came to light at the time.

What's the Aroostookian lesson? It is a classic one about negotiation, really. Sometimes, pragmatically, the offer on the table should be taken, no matter how much it is resented and no matter what the grudges of history might be.

And why is this episode on my mind? Aroostook is, like other rural areas, somewhat more conservative than the urban hubs around it. Due attention paid to this means that somebody – it would be invidious to say who – prevailed in recent office predictions over the re-election of Republican Senator Susan Collins.

CHAPTER 9

THE HOULTON AIRLIFT

We remain in Aroostook County.

The county seat is the small town of Houlton. During the Second World War, before America had entered the war, the USA built an airbase at Houlton, right on the border with Canada. The USA flew planes into the base – careful not to enter Canadian airspace, as the Canadians were and are in the Commonwealth, fighting alongside the British, whilst the USA was 'neutral'. Canadian farmers would then come along with their tractors and literally drag military aircraft over the border. The Canucks would close the highway, which became a temporary runway, and whoosh – off said planes went to London for the war effort.

I love lots about this story. I love the letter of the law being respected and the prompt way around it that was found. I love the fact that it hinged on some local farmers doing their bit. I love the shared endeavour between our three countries in this tiny, obscure corner of cold north Maine.

But there's more. This operation had four casualties, who sadly died in a crash just off the runway when taking a bomber to Britain. The pilot was a Kiwi – yet another nation in this band of friends. So far from home, this is a poignant example of our worldwide shared effort in the most important cause. RIP Royal New Zealand Air Force pilot George Newall Harrison and his radio operator, Royal Canadian Air Force Sergeant Henry Bordewick. Their Commonwealth war graves are maintained in rural Maine to this day by the American Legion. RIP too their comrades RCAF Sergeants August Leroy Beckwall and Arthur Gordon Bartley Gibson, who were buried in their native Canada.

A brace of lessons might be drawn from this story. One might be that with imagination, it's possible to find a route to doing the right thing even whilst working around rules. The second is that one should heed the sacrifices made away from the main stage and the noise of the battlefield. They matter just as much.

CHAPTER 10

THE PRINCE IMPERIAL

In this story we take a look at Napoleon. But not the one you're thinking about.

Louis-Napoléon was the son of Napoleon III, who was the nephew of Napoleon actual 'Napoleon' Napoleon. (Napoleon II was Napoleon's son and didn't live long.) All clear?

Napoleon III was the first President of France, and the last Emperor. That way round, too, rather than the reverse, which might seem more natural. He'd been elected, then couldn't get re-elected, so he seized power. N. III got the Order of the Boot as he led France to ignominious defeat in the Franco-Prussian War of 1870; a ten–nil at home sort of beating. Louis-Napoléon and his parents settled in Chislehurst, in Bromley, which perhaps isn't the most obvious place for exiled European royalty.

Idling along, hoping that Bonapartism at home would prevail and contemplating a suitably grand marriage, Louis-Napoléon – or, after his father's death, Napoleon IV to some – joined the British Army. He was a martial sort, and the French alternative wasn't really open to him at the time. It would be a bold general who sent this young lieutenant into harm's way, given his prospects for the future. Though some cast him as a potential suitor for

Queen Victoria's daughter Beatrice, many in England said that Europe would be better off with him as Emperor of France.

But, as some headstrong young men are wont to do, Louis-Napoléon – or the Prince Imperial, if you like – charmed the usually more sensible women around him into letting him have things his own way. His mother and Queen Victoria herself both intervened to make the army allow him to see action. Thus, the putative future Emperor of France set off for excitement in the Zulu Wars in a lowly lieutenant's garb – and got himself killed in service to England's Queen Empress.

We had assigned him a French-speaker – a Guernseyman named Jahleel Brenton Carey, unjustly blamed for later events – to keep him on the straight and narrow and warn him away from danger, but some simply will not be told. I mean, the lieutenant had strapped Napoleon I's sword from Austerlitz to his side. Destiny called.

It was all his own fault. Louis-Napoléon, Napoleon IV, the Prince Imperial rushed impatiently with a scouting party into disputed territory without waiting for the full complement of men due to be with him. Ostensibly the way was clear...

Ambushed in a kraal in which his small band had stopped whilst they brewed coffee, he was assigned to death by Zulus who were bound to have had firm views on British troops, and possibly on European royalty, but who were unlikely to have appreciated what the skirmish in the middle of nowhere meant for the future of a continent. Indeed, the Zulus sent word that they wouldn't have killed him if they'd known who he was, which was decent of them as he was there in the service of a country with which they were at war and wearing its uniform and so on and so forth. They stressed that he had died bravely – with all his injuries to his front.

His funeral cortège back in Chislehurst for his burial must have been a dreadfully bleak affair. The Bonaparte household had been struck a mortal blow. His mother was devastated; Victoria herself joined the cortège.

Later on, his mother had his body disinterred and placed alongside his father's at St Michael's Abbey, Farnborough, where they remain to this day in the 'Imperial Chapel'. If and when life returns to normal, if you're at the Air Show, you might visit.

There were various manoeuvres made by Frenchmen to bring later Napoleons into play, but with the perspective given by time we now see that the last realistic chance of a return of Bonapartism to France died with Louis-Napoléon in that remote kraal in the summer of 1879.

What's the lesson to be drawn from the tale of Napoleon IV? An easy one, I think. Sometimes, no matter how hot-blooded you are or keen to just get going, when those with more experience than you urge you to wait for a while, then *wait*.

CHAPTER 11

THE CALCUTTA LIGHT HORSE

This is one of my favourite stories from the Second World War, and one of the most unlikely.

Portugal's neutrality was important to Britain. They permitted Allied activity from the Azores, which was vital in combating the German U-boats that threatened the merchant ship lifelines and naval vessels crucial to the war.* Portugal also traded on conspicuously favourable terms with Britain, with whom (then, as now) they shared the oldest continuous alliance in the world. (The UK was careful not to explicitly call on Portugal for help during the war, allowing them to honour both the alliance *and* their neutral status.)

But there was a problem.

In 1942, the Special Operations Executive (SOE) realised that coded messages were being sent to U-boats in the Indian Ocean with precision, allowing the sinking of huge numbers of Allied ships. Portugal's overseas possessions included their colony Goa in India, and a Gestapo spy was detected there. Undercover SOE men went to

---

* Without the use of the base on the Azores that the Portuguese permitted the British to rent, the 'mid-Atlantic gap' in the Allies' ability to provide protection to merchant shipping – a happy Atlantic hunting ground for U-boats which was the object of great dread amongst merchant seaman – would have been much larger. The Azores base didn't close the gap entirely, but it diminished it significantly.

Goa to kidnap him. When they arrived at his home, his wife was unexpectedly there; they kidnapped her too.

This British action was an infringement on Portuguese neutrality, to be sure – just as the spy's presence was in the first place. But snatching a spy was manageable and concealable; the challenge from intelligence that emerged as a result was a rather larger problem. Goa, on the west coast of India, was home to an important harbour: Mormugao. When war was declared, merchant ships from the Axis powers had taken refuge there. For some time this was hardly important. But now, the SOE knew that these ships were transmitting the codes. This wasn't a pair of Gestapo spies to be snatched; there were well-crewed (and rather conspicuously well-defended) ships moored in a neutral harbour. What to do?

The solution was a heady mix of *Boys' Own* adventure and old boys' network that would no doubt attract the disapproval of the modern-day sensitivity reader.* The SOE leading officer on the case happened to know of some old buffers almost 1,400 miles away in Calcutta. The Calcutta Light Horse had been a reserve unit since the Boer War. Like other units 'on reserve' in the Raj, by this point it was a genteel club for rotund chaps in middle age and older who'd nowadays be called 'gammons'.†

Yes, they'd seen service, but that was long ago – the First

---

* Prevalent amongst some publishers and not a made-up term, I'm afraid.

† A pejorative used in British culture for the past decade, the term 'gammon' refers to the supposedly typical flushed face of a person with reactionary views as they express their opinions. Intended to draw a comparison with the pork of the same name, it reflects badly on the person using it as an insult, who'd never otherwise think to use someone's colour as a pejorative.

World War being the most recent. Now, the club's focus was polo – and drinking. On the other hand, they could be trusted; they were keen to do their bit in the war; and they were plausibly deniable. They weren't military now, and who would believe them to be some sort of assault team?

Following the call to help the war effort (without being given any details), the problem was turning away volunteers, not persuading them. Because every single one of the Light Horse volunteered.

The plan was in three parts. First, it called for some of them to cross the entirety of India by rail, north-east to south-west, on various rather flimsy business pretexts. Second, an old barge meant for river work would be sailed from the north-east coast all the way around to Cochin, where it would meet the men and then head up to Goa midway up the west coast. Third, one of their number would go ahead to Goa and put on a party to truly set the town alight. Every sailor in the port would know that a generous old nautical soul had laid on free booze and free prostitutes for all the seamen in town that night. This would get most of the sailors off the boats, the Brits thought.

Then what? Why, it's obvious. The old buffers would sail their barge up to the biggest ship, which they figured held the transmitter, kill the Germans, seize the transmitter and the code books if possible, and sink the ship. If caught, the chaps would chuck their guns overboard and say they were just drunken businessmen up to high jinks, of course.

Each aspect of this plan is plainly preposterous.

It all worked. The boat sank (the crew scuttled in the face of attack). The transmitter was seized (albeit the Germans had successfully burnt the code books). The other German boats, fearing Allied invasion, scuttled themselves too. An Italian ship joined in for good measure. British casualties: none.

U-boat attacks in this arena of war promptly dropped off a cliff.

This action, mucky in terms of neutrality but addressing the covert violation of said neutrality by the other side in the first place, saved hundreds, perhaps thousands, of lives.

Oh, just one more thing, chaps: having come back to service after some decades, pulling off something that few thought could possibly be done – say nothing. Tell no one. The Portuguese wouldn't like it, you see.

And they didn't. For thirty years. They just weren't the sort of men who bragged.

There's a more than serviceable film about this saga, made post-declassification in the '70s, called *The Sea Wolves*. Everyone is in it: Trevor Howard, Gregory Peck, David Niven, Roger Moore. It hacks up some of the story for no reason I can see, but it successfully gets the basics across in an exciting way. The revelatory book *Boarding Party* by James Leasor is superb.

Later still, a bonus emerged in the National Archive records. Three of the Germans declared 'missing' after the action that night had in fact seized the moment to volunteer for the SOE – they came away with the Calcutta Light Horse and served with the British for the rest of the war.

Others amongst the crews of the scuttled ships, under-standably given what post-war Germany was like, stayed in India for the rest of their lives and raised families who are there to this day. When the movie was made, Roger Moore had his family with him. The blonde-haired, blue-eyed Indian family of one of the Germans who'd remained in the country after the war babysat his children during shooting.

The Calcutta Light Horse was, of course, disbanded PDQ after the war and Indian independence. No thanks given; no recognition delivered. I'm sure the Light Horse resented disbandment a great deal; I doubt very much that they cared about the publicity at all.

CHAPTER 12

SOUSA MENDES

We continue the Portuguese theme and remain in the Second World War – but in a rather different vein. Because not every man needs to wield a gun to be a hero; sometimes, a bureaucrat's stamp will do.

Aristides de Sousa Mendes* was the Portuguese consul-general in Bordeaux when France fell to the Nazis in the Second World War. Think of the Paris scenes in *Casablanca*, the last heady days of freedom etc., only in wine country.

Under the Salazar regime, Portugal sought to maintain its neutrality and feared the Axis powers greatly, especially given the Spanish government's closeness to them. It therefore had a very tough set of rules for immigration, as so many people sought to flee the Nazis by getting to the New World or to Allied countries via neutral Portuguese territory.

Lisbon sent all its consuls 'Circular 14', which set out who constituted 'inconvenient or dangerous' refugees and who shouldn't be granted a visa without OK from Lisbon – which, given the pressure, volume and speed required,

---

* Irrelevant side note: Sousa Mendes was a twin with a different birthday to his older brother, as they were born either side of midnight. This must be uncommon, and it made sure that each had his own 'special day' in family celebrations, I suppose.

effectively meant refusing them in most cases. The list included fleeing Jews.

Historians are keen to stress that this was Portugal attempting to avoid danger to itself from the Axis powers and not any sort of ideological point of view. That is correct. Portugal avoided antisemitism more thoroughly than almost anywhere. But in practical terms, this still left thousands fleeing Nazism a great deal worse off.

Sousa Mendes disobeyed the instruction immediately, granting visas without approval from Lisbon, and he soon went further, actively assisting refugees with false passports and forged papers. As the German tanks rolled westwards, demand for help increased – and so did his subterfuge undertaken on behalf of those fleeing.

The day after Marshal Pétain announced that the French should seek an armistice with Germany, Sousa Mendes announced to his family that he would just issue visas to… everybody.

Bordeaux was bombed the next day. Bayonne, on the Spanish border, was packed with refugees. Sousa Mendes went there (happily dodging panicked instructions Lisbon had sent to him at Bordeaux to desist) and relieved the diplomat on duty, who had obediently been refusing visas. Our man had other ideas. Soon he was recalled to Lisbon. He obeyed… rather slowly. Heading back via posts that hadn't heard Lisbon's orders yet and via crossings without telephones, he meandered his way home in his car, granting visas and waving refugees over the borders wherever he went.

He was punished once he finally got home, of course. His pay was docked, his career was effectively ended, his family was shunned by Portuguese society. After the war, Salazar claimed credit for his country for all the refugees it had accepted. This was understandable and had some truth to it – but perhaps rather more recognition belonged to someone else. Sousa Mendes today is honoured as righteous amongst the nations, rescuer of thousands from the Nazis.

None of this is meant to be criticism of the UK's oldest ally – the oldest alliance anyone has had, anywhere, ever. We are lucky to have such friends. It's just to say that, sometimes, unlikely people are the most wonderful heroes, civil servants included. Aristides Sousa Mendes was such a one.

What's the lesson? Sometimes, you are definitely going to be punished for doing what you know to be right. You should still do it. The arc of history may be long and so on and so forth.

CHAPTER 13

YOU ARE NOT TO FEEL BAD ABOUT THIS

Gavin Ewart was a poet. He was rated highly by Philip Larkin, which I find a pretty infallible recommendation in such things. He wrote wittily and funnily and talked a lot about sex.*

I concede, before the left shouts it, that looking back at his time at Cambridge he wrote that our country was smug, half-alive and semi-Fascist – both before and after the Second World War. Perhaps today he'd have #FBPE (follow back pro-EU) in his Twitter bio.

Ewart served his country in the Royal Artillery in the Second World War (like my step-grandfather). A precociously published author pre-war, he found that he could not write during the war, nor for a long time after it. But he eventually returned to poetry and national fame, and he was prolific in his later years.

Anyway, Nigel Spivey of the *Financial Times* met Ewart, then seventy-nine, at the Café Royal for an instalment of the famous 'Lunch with the *FT*' series of interviews. The *FT* reports that the main item had was alcohol. Ewart began with several negronis and pushed on in similar style. Late in the afternoon, the men finally poured themselves

---

*   I confess that I hadn't read his poetry particularly widely until after I initially published this story online. After that, I went away and read more. A lot of it is filthy!

36

unsteadily out of the restaurant and went their separate ways. Spivey reports that the following day he received a call from Mrs Ewart: 'There are two things you need to know. The first is that Gavin came home yesterday happier than I have seen him in a long time. The second – and you are not to feel bad about this – is that he died this morning.'

Of course, it's a point about a life well lived and a good death; but really, it's a vignette about the magnificent and kind and thoughtful Mrs Ewart, isn't it?

Postscript. This tale put me in mind of a story from Ed Murrow's American radio programme *This I Believe*, reported by Kate Chisholm of *The Spectator*. It is a quotation from a housewife from Virginia whose husband dropped dead after laughing with her at a joke she had just made: 'Louise, you gorgeous fool,' he said. 'And then he died.'

CHAPTER 14

PRINCE ROY OF SEALAND

This is the story of Prince Roy, and – no matter how far-fetched it sounds – it is true.

Roy Bates was British, to begin with. He served his country in the Second World War and, as this chapter will show, later served his own realm. His jaw was shattered by a German bomb before he married a beauty queen.

Having recovered from his war injuries and married the girl of his dreams, Roy became a pirate radio host. And it was thus that he came to see the attraction of abandoned offshore Maunsell Sea Forts, which were awkward for the authorities to police. In the Second World War, said forts were built, as the name implies, in the sea to protect our east coast ports and the entrance to the Thames Estuary. Some might think them bleak, windswept, oil-rig type affairs. But to Roy, they were the promised land.

He first set up shop on Knock John Fort, which is about 9 nautical miles off the coast of Essex. But soon his eyes were upon a greater prize – HM Fort Roughs. Roughs is 6 nautical miles off the coast of Suffolk. Pay attention to the distance, as it's important.

In 1966, Roy seized Fort Roughs with fellow adventurer Ronan O'Rahilly (who ran Radio Caroline), ejecting earlier pirate broadcaster occupants. But the town wasn't big enough for the both of them. Roy soon booted Ronan out, too.

O'Rahilly rounded up some toughs and attempted to retake Fort Roughs in 1967. But our Roy was having none of it. With guns and petrol bombs these pretenders were swiftly repelled.

Disquieted by events, HM Royal Marines and Royal Navy attended upon Roughs. But Roy's son, Prince Michael, persuaded these usurpers to abandon their approach with warning shots. For these waters were now, they claimed, theirs. The forts had been abandoned outside UK territorial waters – HM Roughs was now 'The Principality of Sealand'. And they were entitled to defend it. Both noble Princes of Sealand were arrested by UK police and charged with firearms offences. But, hurrah, these charges were dismissed! For, as the court wisely realised, these were international affairs beyond the UK's territorial limits. Plainly, Prince Roy maintained, this was not only vindication in a court of law with regard to the piddling false charges their highnesses faced – moreover, it amounted to recognition of his new country. Whether or not anyone else called it that (spoiler: they didn't), he was entitled to behave as such now. Modesty alone can explain why he took the title 'Prince' and not 'King'.

Sealand started issuing passports PDQ. Rather a lot of them. More, in fact, than might plausibly be thought to represent the population of a small platform at sea. It took for itself an anthem, a flag and so on. The sort of thing that new groups do when they are pretending to be a country.

Sadly, the police charges were not the end of the young principality's troubles. A German businessman, Alexander Achenbach, sought in 1978 to engineer a deal with Prince Roy in which a luxury hotel and casino would be erected in the realm. It did not come off, and Achenbach did not take failure well.

Styling himself Prime Minister of Sealand, this treacherous dog lured Prince Roy away from the principality on a false business lead and hired Dutch and German mercenaries to help him conquer Sealand in a putsch in Roy's absence. Storming the kingdom by jet ski, speedboat and helicopter, they took control and took Prince Michael hostage. An outrage!

But such insurrectionists were no match for Prince Roy. He had served his first country at Monte Cassino! These mercenary running dogs were as nothing by comparison. They had underestimated him and his family – for none knew the secrets of Sealand like Prince Roy. Hiring a helicopter of his own, our gallant hero regained access to his land, and to a cache of weapons he had hidden therein. Said weapons were promptly deployed, in no uncertain terms. Prince Michael was freed and the aggressors were tamed; peace was restored in the land.

But this was no mere case of foreign hostility; it was treason, for Achenbach was the holder of a Sealand passport! The rest of the invaders were released, but Achenbach was righteously imprisoned in Sealand's highest tower.*

---

* It doesn't have one, but you know what I mean.

Hanging would have been too good for such a one. Truly, it shows Prince Roy's graciousness that rather than the swift execution that was so evidently merited, he merely kept the insurrectionist as his prisoner and began negotiations with his equals in Germany for the fiend's release.

Negotiate, Germany did. This, again, was surely evidence that Prince Roy's sovereign claims were true. By the grace of Roy, Achenbach was released and returned to Germany – only for him to claim to be the head of a government in exile, the Sealand Rebel Government! Why, Iago had nothing on this one.

Totally coincidentally, it was also in 1987 that Britain extended its territorial waters claim from 3 miles to 12. The principality was now claimed to be in the UK's waters. Clearly this was motivated by Britain's concerns about the rising power of mighty Sealand. Yes, every country everywhere recognised Britain's claim to Sealand under the laws of the sea, but what did such details matter?

Neither the manoeuvring of the pretender Achenbach nor the claims of authority over Sealand by other states were obstacles to the principality's success. Internet domain schemes flourished. Passport sales – ahem, accreditation to loyal new citizens – carried on at a steady clip. Stamps, coins, peerages granted online... there was no end to Sealand's bounty.

But then, alas, the realm was struck with tragedy upon tragedy.

A fire broke out in 2006 and, as a percentage of territory damaged, it was surely the worst event ever to happen to any country, rendering much of Sealand a blighted waste. And then, in 2012... Prince Roy died.

Prince Michael had reigned for some time as prince regent, as Prince Roy was unwell – but still, the founder leader's passing seemed a mortal blow to the principality's energies. The following year, a Sealand flag was planted on Everest. Poignant, but little recompense.

Sealand carries on today, its prince reigning in absentia as he runs a cockle fishing business in Leigh-on-Sea. Sports teams remain accredited. Film rights to the tale are discussed. But one fears things can never be the same without the magnificent major, the much-lamented late Prince Roy.

CHAPTER 15

GEORGE H. W. BUSH

George H. W. Bush was the 41st President of the USA and father of the 43rd. To the modern audience, perhaps he's best known as author of the classiest letter to a successor to have become public. But there's much more of him to be known.

The last President to serve his country in combat, he was a navy pilot, serving with distinction in the Second World War, flying fifty-eight combat missions and receiving three Air Medals and the Distinguished Flying Cross for heroism and extraordinary achievement. After the war, he was successful in the oil industry, relocating his family to Texas.

Then came politics. He was a member of the US House of Representatives for Texas and US ambassador to the United Nations. He chaired the Republican National Committee, which was perhaps not quite the bunfight it is now but was still an undertaking of significance. He was the USA's most senior diplomat in China (effectively the ambassador, but this was prior to the restoration of formal Sino-US diplomatic relations). He was the director of the CIA. He served as Vice-President to President Reagan for two terms.

Last of all, he was President when the Berlin Wall fell

and the communist regimes were dismantled, and he successfully brought together an international coalition against Saddam Hussein in response to the invasion of Kuwait.

So, in my view, he was perhaps the most well credentialed and experienced man in public life in our time.[*]

Towards the end of this life of public service, he was asked in an interview to reflect on this record and say what had made him most proud. He thought about the question, and then said with certainty: 'My children still want to come home.'

One more story. Former Presidents still have a Secret Service detail. One of Bush's guards had a little boy with leukaemia. In sympathy and love, Bush's detail all shaved their heads for their comrade. They turned up for duty the next day. Former President Bush had shaved his head.

---

[*] None of this stopped him losing his final election to Bill Clinton, rendering him one of the few Presidents to serve only one term in office. I daresay you can name another more recent one.

CHAPTER 16

DIANA ROWDEN

Diana Rowden served in the Women's Auxilliary Air Force (WAAF) and then the Special Operations Executive (SOE). She died in a concentration camp when she was twenty-nine years old, when the Nazis executed her.

I championed Rowden's cause in a recent balloon debate online with the Conservative Women's Organisation. I lost, coming second to Edwina Currie, who had chosen Margaret Thatcher. That outcome may very well seem to you to be predictable. But despite my defeat, let me tell you about my candidate and why I chose her.

Educated in part in Surrey, in part in Italy and in part on the French Riviera, she was a young British patriot who knew part of occupied Europe well, and her French was excellent – making her a tremendous intelligence asset in the making.

But the state didn't come to her; she volunteered. First, she volunteered for the Red Cross and was serving with them on the Continent when France fell to the Third Reich. Cut off by the Allied collapse in 1940, it took her much of 1941 to be able to escape back to Britain via Spain and Portugal. Second, once home, she undertook intelligence work with the WAAF, securing rapid promotion. Third and finally, in 1943, she signed up with the SOE.

Rowden was now a British spy, working for our intelligence service and for the resistance in occupied France. Her instructors' reports tell us that she was a good shot and an excellent grenade thrower. It seems to me that we need a few more good grenade throwers in life right now.

She worked as a courier, conveying secret messages between Britain and the network of resistance fighters in France. But, after a short and event-and-explosives-filled period behind enemy lines, she and many colleagues were betrayed by a double agent. Thereafter, she was on the run.

After her cover had been blown, she went 'into hiding' with a French family, though she would take the children of the family tobogganing every morning.

She was ultimately captured and imprisoned with other brave women like her, and those who survived say she buoyed up those with her with cheerful spirits until her last day.

So, I think that she is a great representative for women being heroines and doing their bit for their country as equals to men. But when I began my research into who I should champion for that debate, I didn't know who Diana Rowden was. When you read her name in this book, chances are you didn't know it either. There is a campaign run by my friend Zehra Zaidi for greater recognition of our brave SOE women, and I proudly endorse it.

Rowden was brave and patriotic. It seems to me that we could do with bravery and a bit of patriotism right now. In a time when we reward blandness, shouldn't we celebrate someone who chose her accommodation based on whether she could leg it from the roof without being seen? Indeed, who better to champion than someone best known for blowing up a Peugeot factory? To varying degrees, the others whose stories I've told in this book now have the fame they've earned. To this day, Diana Rowden does not.

CHAPTER 17

JAN MASARYK

Jan Masaryk was the son of the founding President of Czechoslovakia. Coincidentally, his civil service career really took off after his dad took office.

He was posted to the Czechoslovakian Embassy in the USA after the First World War. Then, he became aide to the Foreign Secretary (Edvard Beneš, who succeeded his father as President). Then, he became the long-standing Czechoslovakian ambassador to the UK.

Whilst in the UK, he became Foreign Minister in the Czechoslovakian government-in-exile during the Second World War. When the conflict had finished, he returned to his country, which was under Soviet occupation of course, and stayed in that role – remaining in it after a Czechoslovakian communist government formed in 1946.

In 1948, some of the non-communists in government tried to force new elections by resigning. They failed. Masaryk was the only non-communist or fellow traveller in a prominent public role, and he was therefore useful to the Soviets and their puppets... and then when he endorsed the idea of Czechoslovakia taking money from the hated West under the Marshall Plan, he suddenly wasn't.

Conveniently for some, supposedly he promptly committed suicide, jumping from a window in his official apartment in the baroque Czernin Palace in Prague, to which he'd been confined (with a whole new set of staff) since his Marshall Plan outburst.

There were, let's say, reasons for scepticism about this suicide explanation. Amongst them, I'd count the following points. There were scratch marks around the window frame, consistent with, er, someone desperately clinging to life against someone trying to chuck them out of it. Witnesses had passed through the courtyard below the window a quarter of an hour before his body was found in it – and you might think they'd notice a body splayed out on the cobbles; they didn't. However, the police doctor who carried out the preliminary examination ruled that his death had taken place at least *two hours* prior. Masaryk's own doctor was not allowed to attend the post-mortem. The doctor who undertook it had demonstrated his willingness to work flexibly with unpleasant regimes by being a long-standing servant of the Nazis.

Masaryk supposedly jumped from a small, narrow window set high up in the wall – hard to get to; hard to get through. His own bedroom window in the palace was large and much easier to get through. He apparently chose this tough and unpleasant route to die, ignoring the gun and the drugs easily available to him in his chambers.

Some members of his family maintained that there was no way that Masaryk would take his own life. He revered his father and spent his whole life trying to live up to his example. His father had famously decried suicide as a coward's way of escape. And if it was in fact suicide, then it would be the second definitely-not-defenestration death by jumping from a window by an awkward government minister, as the former Minister of Justice had done just the same – or not – recently before.

Columbo would be saying, 'Just one more thing' all over this case, wouldn't he?

Little wonder that, with the dark humour so prevalent amongst those enduring communist regimes, the joke in Czechoslovakia was that Masaryk was a man so tidy-minded he'd even closed the windows behind himself after he jumped.

A second inquiry, after the Prague Spring of 1968, concluded that the incident was an accident but didn't rule out murder. After the communist regimes in the East fell in the 1990s, a third inquiry held – surprise! – that he was murdered. A fourth inquiry, by the police in the 2000s, ditto.

But... by whom?

So much has been revealed and unexplained incidents finally understood by personal testimony and archive material becoming available after the fall of communism. But, despite the case being so high-profile in his country, Masaryk's death isn't amongst them. His murder remains unsolved to this day.

The police re-re-re-reopened the case at the end of 2019 on government instructions; no findings yet – coronavirus has no doubt stymied progress and so on and so forth. So, for the first time in this book – watch this space.

The motto of Czechoslovakia at the time – under the

communists and before it peaceably split in two after independence – was 'Truth Prevails'. The memorial plaque to Masaryk in Prague's Vila Osvěta bears an interesting addition to this slogan: 'The truth prevails – but it takes some elbow grease.'

And so it shall be here.

CHAPTER 18

JAN PALACH

For Chapter 18, we stay in Prague and with a Jan. Jan Palach was twenty years old when he set himself on fire.

In 1968, the Prague Spring took place. Alexander Dubček became First Secretary of the Communist Party of Czechoslovakia; he was a reformist, and hopes amongst those desiring more liberalisation were high. Such hopes weren't misplaced – as far as Dubček was concerned.

Unfortunately, they were doomed with the Soviets. Dubček began lessening restrictions on the media and speech, on travel and the economy. Such things were embraced in Czechoslovakia by people willing him on, but it was all too much for Moscow, and in August, Warsaw Pact forces swiftly occupied the country to restore the old order. Acts of resistance were many but on a small scale. Genuine fighting at scale was never going to happen. How, when so overwhelmingly outgunned, does one resist?

In Prague's New Town (established, please note, American friends, in 1348), Wenceslas Square is a busy centre. It was here that Palach self-immolated in protest at the repression of his country. Imagine the pain. And the bravery. I'm not sure that I can fully grasp either.

The impact that people can have on our world is not dictated by the length of the lives they lived. I find it

impossible to contemplate Palach's sacrifice without realising selfishly that I'm twice as old as he was when he
made it.

It took Palach several days to die. He talked a little in
that time. Doctors said he told them that he did what he
did not so much against the Soviets as such, but rather so
as to inspire his countrymen to rise from their demoralised
acceptance of what the Soviets were doing. If this is so, it
worked. The twentieth anniversary of Palach's death saw
marches and demonstrations repressed by the police even
in the dying days of communism. Some Czechoslovakians
saw the harsh attacks on protesters during 'Palach Week'
as a tipping point in the decisive shift of their country
away from communism.

The Second World War was won by the right side, but
it had uneven outcomes. One repressive, evil regime was
defeated, but another continued in power for decades. The
Czechoslovakians and many others lived under it for gen-
erations in the twentieth century.

Palach was not the only person to self-immolate, not
even in that country and not even just during that period
of repression. But it is right to say that this young man
stood as a symbol for the desire for freedom that eventually, after so much loss, prevailed.

CHAPTER 19

THE DIE HARDS

Die Hard is the best Christmas film. This truism is well known. But the phrase 'die hard' actually has a much longer history.

In the early 1800s, Spain and Portugal fought the Peninsular War against the invading / occupying French. As usual in any given scrap in the past millennium or so, the British were on board against the French.

At the Battle of Albuera, quite near the Spanish / Portuguese border, in 1811, a combined British, German, Spanish and Portuguese force fought Napoleon's Armée du Midi (which included some Poles, from the Duchy of Warsaw). In sum: heavy losses on both sides; result, a score draw.* Such conclusions belie the human stories of the encounter.

Major General Daniel Hoghton was a national hero to the British. Two thirds of his brigade died in the line at Albuera, including Hoghton himself (Wellington noted that he had been waving his hat to encourage his men forward at the moment he fell). The French had out-positioned

---

* There were 7,640 British infantrymen at Albuera; 4,159 were made casualties. This appalling loss of life rendered Beresford, the British commander, utterly despondent. Wellington arrived at Albuera three days after the battle and ordered Beresford to rewrite his report of the battle to suggest that it had been a victory rather than reflecting the despair he exhibited in his first draft. He rewrote it.

them, able to 'enfilade' (fire along their longest axis) with a devastating hail of grapeshot and canister (like huge shotguns).

Colonel William Inglis, one of the many Scots to have flourished during Empire, commanded the 57th Regiment of Foot, part of Hoghton's Brigade. He had joined it as an ensign and served with it since the American Revolutionary War in 1781. So, we can imagine how it felt for him to see the 57th, his home and his family for his entire adult life, massacred under him. Early on, a piece of four-pound grapeshot had gone through his neck and lodged in his back. This isn't good for you. He refused to leave the field, staying with his regiment's colours as the battle raged and his line shrunk back towards him.

As he lay dying (as he and others would have thought), he called out to his beloved men, again and again: 'Die hard, 57th – die hard.'

For he and they would have thought that this time was the end of them. All that was left was the question of how they died. ('As if the way one falls down matters!' 'When the fall is all that's left, it matters.')* But surrounding their colonel, facing their end, the 57th fought ferociously, their concentrated fire repelling the French until they were finally relieved by other British forces. By then, fully three quarters of the 57th had fallen.

Inglis became famous for his cry, and the 57th became known as 'The Die Hards'. Inglis could not be operated

---

* *The Lion in Winter*, Haworth Productions, 1968.

upon until two days after the battle (imagine the metal lodged in your body for two days). But he ultimately recovered, fought in the Peninsula again, was made a Knight Commander of the Order of the Bath and in retirement was made colonel of the regiment in which he'd served for over thirty years.

The true story of die hard.

CHAPTER 20

THE DAY OF THE TILES

We have all – until these recent, housebound times – enjoyed the occasional 'night on the tiles'. But the Day of the Tiles was quite different and (depending on how you spend your nights, I suppose) rather more painful.

The ancient city of Grenoble was the capital of the old, proud French region of Dauphiné in the south-east of that country. (Possession of the region by French royalty came with the condition that the heir to the throne be called '*Dauphin*' after it. There's an obvious parallel with our title 'Prince of Wales'.) Louis XVI did not have a good run of things, what with being the only French monarch to be executed, presiding over the end of more than a thousand years of royal rule and so on. But he could hardly have appreciated that things would kick off in the way they did in the south-eastern corner of the realm at Grenoble.

The people of Dauphiné were impoverished by France's ongoing financial crisis. Harvests were bad. Bread was expensive. The first (clerical) and second (aristocratic) estates indicated no willingness to give up privileges. So, the third (peasant and bourgeois) looked to take things into their own hands.

As is so often the way with new movements, they sought to ground their demands in the heritage of an older tradition, so as to lend their position credibility and authority. Thus, the old Estates of the Province of Dauphiné would serve as the pretext for their gathering of proto-republican sentiment.

Locked in a headlong death spiral of absolutism and short-sighted self-interest, both the Crown and the nobles and clergymen in orbit around it refused to yield an inch on anything. (Nowadays they'd have been spinning the notion that they were in 'listening mode' and perhaps initiating an interminable judge-led inquiry, and the *ancien régime* might well have survived.) So it was that the Crown sent troops to Grenoble to quell this movement, and things came to a head on 7 June 1788.

There are good reasons not to put troops on the streets at times of concern about law and order. Not only is there a vital distinction between the civilian populace policing itself and the army imposing law upon it – between civil and martial law – but also there is the point that once the army is deployed, it does what it does. Armies are for fighting.

Thus it was that as the elite regiment of the Royal Navy sought to suppress protesters, the sight of one of them bayonetting an old man spurred the growing crowds to fury. Small groups of troops, outnumbered by the mass of revolting citizens of Grenoble and otherwise unable to carry out their orders to take control, opened fire into the crowds.

Many rioters took to the rooftops of buildings on the streets down which the soldiers were seeking to quell dissent. A rain of rooftiles from all sides soon assailed the forces of the Crown – hence 'Day of the Tiles'.

Such circumstances are all but impossible for law enforcement. The mob out of control cannot be reasoned with, but it is made up of their fellow Frenchmen, whose demands they might share on another day. The troops gradually yielded control of much of the town to the mob (but not the arsenal; never the arsenal). The judges who were due to attend the meeting of the estates, and whose potential departure from Grenoble had most proximately precipitated the uprising, were pressed back to the palace by a crowd carrying flowers and singing the praises of Parliament.

The army, realising it was on to a loser, gave permission for the estates to meet as long as that meeting took place outside the city at the beautiful Château de Vizille, today home of the Museum of the French Revolution. The compromise was canny and astute, albeit the authority the army possessed to offer it might have been rather elusive.

These events therefore constituted both the first violent outbreak in what became the French Revolution and its first public meetings, which saw demands for both a national Parliament and an end to absolute monarchy – a movement which changed Europe. So, it's worth knowing about the 'Day of the Tiles'.

Three postscripts. First: it's amazing how much people preferred not to blame the monarchy for France's predicament, instead holding supposedly bad servants of the Crown responsible. The crowds at Grenoble even sang praises to the King during their protests. Even at this point, Louis could have rescued things with a different approach.

Second: in a coup, seize the airport and the radio station. In a French anti-monarchic protest, seize the cathedral. The crowd rang the bells of the cathedral in a signal for the peasantry around Grenoble to come to their aid and join in the riot. I think the symbolism potent.

Finally: my interest in this tale was spurred by Rafael Sabatini's enjoyable historical novel *Scaramouche*, which, to the disappointment of some, is not the novelisation of 'Bohemian Rhapsody'.

CHAPTER 21

GORDIEVSKY AND RUDENESS

In these challenging times, people are understandably reflecting on the past and realising that there are things in their lives that they regret. Looking back, I realise that I was insufficiently rude to two people. One of them was Geoffrey Howe.

I partially owe that conclusion, and this story, to the brilliant *The Spy and the Traitor* by Ben Macintyre, which you should read. In the dark days of Soviet Russia, Oleg Gordievsky was a double agent, spying for Britain for a generation. He was blown almost certainly because of a traitor in the CIA. In 1985, ominously, he was summoned to return to Russia without explanation. Whilst he thought that he had *probably* been discovered, he still went back to Moscow from London (where he could have claimed asylum and all would have been fine) because...

1) there was a chance he had not been blown;

2) there were more secrets potentially to be had by behaving as if everything was fine, which it just *might* be, having whatever meetings Moscow wanted and then getting back into post in London; and

3) he was one of the bravest men the world has ever seen.

But it wasn't fine.

The KGB, having promptly detained, drugged and questioned him and shown their hand, wrongly tried to play a long game in order to get more evidence of guilt and bring in others to whom he might be connected, letting him go home to his flat (which was bugged) and so on. They were trying to break him down slowly. It might take time, they reasoned, but they were sure of their position because nobody had ever escaped the USSR. This was logical, but false, confidence.

First, Gordievsky managed to give his signal to the MI6 / diplomatic team at the UK's Moscow Embassy that he was going to try to escape Russia. A plan for this had been in place for years, with carefully selected and quietly briefed individuals amongst the British diplomats posted to Moscow accustomed to walking, week after week after week for the entirety of their time in Russia, past certain places at certain times with distinctive carrier bags and confectionery as the signal to a man they'd likely never actually meet that they were always there to protect him.

But having a plan is different to executing it.

To carry out the task, to rescue this man who had done so much for us, action needed to be signed off at the highest level. Regrettably, Geoffrey Howe was at the highest level and said, gosh, it all sounds like it could be a bit awkward with the Russians; sod him, he can die.

Fortunately, above the highest level is the Thatcher tier. Margaret Thatcher said, well, thanks for that, Geoffrey, but this man has helped to prevent nuclear war and served the democratic West my whole political life. We are going to get him, and we are going to bring him home.

Hence the famously risky border crossing into Finland with Gordievsky in the boot of a diplomat's car, with said diplomat's wife changing the nappy of said diplomat's baby on top of the boot to put off the sniffer dogs (which worked). No thanks to Geoffrey Howe, Oleg Gordievsky is alive and well somewhere in the UK today.

Howe was a bencher of my Inn of Court, Middle Temple – one of various great institutions I've been lucky enough to drift through. I met him and loathed him for his anti-Thatcherism, but, callow youth as I was, I failed to voice it beyond evincing general surliness, and I now realise that I had all the more reason to. For shame.

Still, I am reminded by the always excellent barrister and legal guru Jeremy Brier that, on the all too few occasions I attended Hall at Middle Temple, upon the toast to 'absent friends' I would always bellow, in the silence as everyone else was dutifully sipping, 'EXCEPT GEOF-FREY HOWE.' So there's that, at least.*

The other person I was insufficiently rude to was Edward Heath. That's a story that can wait for another day.

---

* As, unlike me, Brier went on from our qualifying days to have an extremely successful legal career, I should stress that this was all down to me and not him. He was present but not involved.

CHAPTER 22

THE ANTARCTIC APPENDIX

If you are of a squeamish disposition, look away now. Don't say I didn't warn you.

Leonid Rogozov served as the doctor on the 6th Soviet Antarctic Expedition from September 1960 to October 1962. This expedition established the (deep breath) Novolazarevskaya Station, which sits on the Schirmacher Oasis – an example of nominative false advertising if ever there was one.

The expedition had come by ship from Russia. The journey had taken over a month, and the ship would not be back to pick them up for a year. Setting up the base was OK; winter had struck by February, which is no small thing in the Antarctic, and the dozen men hunkered down to see it out, hoping not to recreate John Carpenter's *The Thing*, no doubt.

On 29 April, Rogozov started to feel sick. This was bad. He was the only person in the group with medical training. His general fatigue and dizziness particularised soon enough into pain on his right side and peritonitis became apparent. It was his appendix.

Diagnosis easy; treatment hard. They were 1,000 miles from even theoretical help (Mirny, another Soviet station);

the closer stations were held by other powers and reported that they had no aircraft available, and a heavy blizzard meant that they couldn't have landed even if the aircraft existed.

He didn't have any choice. The 27-year-old junior doctor Rogozov would have to operate on himself.

This is hard to contemplate, and hard to do in and of itself. But it was harder yet in his case because he was nauseous – and he was getting worse, fast. He injected a little novocaine in his gut as local anaesthetic, propped himself up with a small mirror *Master and Commander* style, and took a scalpel to his own abdomen.

I think that we will forgive a man operating in these conditions for making a mistake. He made one: he cut into his intestine and had to sew it back up before going on. No more anaesthetic, by the way – he needed a clear head and still had a 5in. hole in his side with a dodgy appendix behind it.

Still with me?

Rogozov was increasingly nauseous and weak, frequently requiring rest breaks to recover. But he went on and cut out his own appendix. It was black at the base and would have burst imminently. He then stitched himself up.

He wasn't alone, of course. His colleagues were with him, passing instruments to him on demand and with instructions on the adrenaline shot they were to give him if he passed out, so he could carry on. It wasn't needed. (Charmingly, he wrote later about his concern, as he operated on himself, for *their* well-being as they looked on, as they were so pale and terrified.)*

Rogozov was back to work within two weeks, received the Order of the Red Banner of Labour the same year and worked until his death in 2000 as head of surgery at the St Petersburg Research Institute for Tubercular Pulmonology (he went back to work at the hospital the day after getting back from Antarctica).

What's the lesson to be taken from the Soviet surgeon? Well, the next time you feel like you're having a bad day, imagine how Rogozov felt the day he looked down at his gut and realised, as the Antarctic blizzard howled outside, what the swelling and pain meant he'd have – despite his fever – to do to himself.

---

* This echoes my, from many, many possibilities, very favourite scene from *Master and Commander* – the film in most dire need of a sequel of any film – as Maturin asks the surprisingly squeamish Aubrey if *he* is alright as Maturin operates on himself.

CHAPTER 23

WHAT IS THE ONE CITY...?

'Don't pub-quiz me,' the Labour former shadow minister Emily Thornberry once famously declared to an interviewer who had the temerity to ask her about a statistic. Unusually for someone renowned for being so closely in tune with the mood of the British public, this was an off note from Thornberry, as we love a pub quiz. Today's quiz question is: what's the only city to have been a European capital that is *not* in Europe?

The answer is Rio de Janeiro, and the explanation continues our occasional Portuguese #deanehistory theme. Napoleon's push into Iberia in what became known as the Peninsular War (and which gave us the Die Hards) was going worryingly well – if you were a member of the Portuguese nobility, anyway. In 1807, the Portuguese monarchy, fearing the worst, had decamped from Lisbon to Brazil. They made Rio de Janeiro, some 5,000 miles away, capital of Portugal. Poor old Rio isn't even the capital of Brazil any longer (another pub quiz favourite – it's Brasilia, of course, which I *always* typo as Brazilia as that was the name of the nightclub in my home town). But for a time there Rio was capital to both Portugal and Portuguese America.

When the war was over, there were understandable calls

for the monarchy to return home. Surely the realm could not permanently be run from a colony? The problem was that everyone at court... really rather liked Rio. King John VI therefore promptly upgraded Brazil to a kingdom. So there! It wasn't a monarchy running things in Portugal from a colony after all. Long live the United Kingdom of Portugal, Brazil and the Algarves! What a holiday destination sweep title.

Unsurprisingly perhaps, nobody bought this. You've got to come back, John. We are Portugal. You run Portugal. That's how it works. John dragged things out, but in the end, facing a potential revolution at home no less, a mere seven years after the close of hostilities in the Peninsular War, the court returned to Lisbon.

John left his son Prince Pedro to lead things in Brazil as regent. Pedro took this responsibility for leading Brazil's future rather more seriously than his father might have expected. A year after John left, he declared Brazil independent, restyled himself Emperor, established his capital at... Rio and generally waved two fingers towards faraway Europe and faraway father.

The lesson from this story is that daddy issues play an often underestimated part in the fates of nations. (Lest I be accused of twisting facts for a punchline, I acknowledge that history shows Pedro hated his mother far more.)

CHAPTER 24

THE FAMILY STORY

This is the story of Jonas Noreika, and of his granddaughter, Silvia Foti. It is a story of the past and of the present.

After the Second World War, Jonas Noreika led the Lithuanian revolt against the USSR, of 1945–46. The Russians executed him. His name rings out; in some ways, he has served as the embodiment of that proud country's post-war national story. Streets bear his name. There is a Jonas Noreika school.

Foti was brought up in the United States, and she was raised to revere the memory of the man whose portrait hung in her home. The Lithuanian expatriate community around her must have thought this little girl blessed to be descended from such a man.

On her deathbed, Foti's mother turned to her daughter – now a journalist – and asked her to take up the great family project: a book about her grandfather that would really tell his story, authenticate the legend and serve to preserve it for ever more. What an honour she must have felt this to have been.

So, we can picture the moment in the archives when Foti turned from one page to another and turned her family's life over with it; the moment she turned to the page from 1941 upon which her grandfather's signature was written under the order to round up the Jews.

By his order, the Lithuanian Jews in his region were sent to the ghettoes and thence to the camps. Between those two hells, we now know, almost all of them died. Yes, the Nazis drove this scheme of human slaughter. But some Lithuanians had been complicit – Foti's grandfather foremost amongst them. Not just complicit, either. Noreika didn't 'just' sign a form or two (as if such signatures alone don't kill). As Foti read on and dug deeper, she saw the extent to which her grandfather was an antisemite himself, who had greatly benefited from his closeness to the occupying regime.

Pause to imagine the moment in Foti's life that this must have been – the bifurcation; everything before it, and everything after it. To think that some say history doesn't matter. There must have been a dark moment of the soul. The temptation to put her research in a drawer must have been very strong. That we know all this tells you what she determined to do – as does the existence of her book, *The Nazi's Granddaughter*. Foti has been castigated by the Lithuanian émigré world in which she was raised, and by her ancestral homeland too. It is one of the bravest publications of our time and gives us a tough and worthwhile Cromwellian lesson: speak the truth, warts and all.

CHAPTER 25

KARPOV VS KORCHNOI VS DEATH RAYS VS HYPNOTISM

We turn to the chessboard in this story. It works for Netflix; why not for us? (There will definitely be no chess moves in this story, and definitely no pieces sliding on ceilings, and probably no wild binge drinking.)

In the most famous chess match in history, Bobby Fischer of the USA beat Boris Spassky of the USSR to win the world championships in Reykjavík in 1972, at the height of the Cold War. But, having won, the mercurial Fischer refused to defend his title in the next championships.

He had conditions (or rather, demands) for any title defence that the regulatory body would not grant; that was the premise on which he walked away. Whether in truth it was that dispute that motivated him, or that having scaled the heights he couldn't or wouldn't repeat the feat, he won one and was done. The Sam Allardyce of chess.*

Normally, there would be a competition between challengers (or 'candidates') to take on the champion. The

---

* Allardyce has the presumably never-to-be-beaten record as England manager of 100 per cent wins – his side won one game (against Slovakia, in injury time) before he gave up his position by mutual agreement, after he was the subject of a newspaper 'sting' about circumventing third-party player ownership rules. This is a very witty pop culture reference.

candidates' round took place as planned in 1974. Anatoly Karpov won that and became the champion by default, given the prodigy Fischer's newly found Greta Garbo approach to public appearances.

So it was that, in 1978, Karpov had to 'defend' his title without having won it.

To be clear, Karpov had done some hard yards in the candidates' tournament. But it always mattered to Karpov (and his critics) that he didn't win the title from Fischer – the fact that it was forfeited to him stung hard. The 1978 championship – the first for a whole six years since the Icelandic affair – was fought in Baguio in the Philippines, between two Russians. But these Russians could not have been more different. The biggest contrasts between the men and their camps weren't about chess. They were about politics and personality.

Karpov, in his late twenties, was a model Soviet. He had cruised to the top of the chess world without a setback (barring the inability to beat Fischer for the title, which was no fault of his). A staunch Communist Party member and happy Muscovite, he was the golden boy of the USSR. His opponent, Viktor Korchnoi, was in his late forties. He had qualified for the candidates' tournament on no fewer than five occasions; now his big chance had finally come. Korchnoi was ever rebellious and outspoken, and he felt sidelined by the regime's very clear preferment of Karpov as the face of the game.

The Russians felt, and said, that the generation which had been beaten by Fischer was not the one to take up the championship pursuit for the future. When Korchnoi had made some spiteful comments about Karpov after his ascension, the Soviets had banned him from tournament play for a year. In 1976, Korchnoi was permitted to compete at a tournament in Amsterdam, probably in order to show the chess world that Karpov would face strong enough competition later to merit calling him world champion. After the tournament, which he won jointly along with Englishman Tony Miles, Korchnoi wandered into a Dutch police station and declared to the no doubt bemused desk officer that he wished to seek asylum.

(Irrelevant side note: the story goes that straight after the tournament, as far as his minders were concerned Korchnoi was deeply discussing post-match analysis with Miles; he was in fact getting Miles to teach him how to spell 'political asylum'.)

Rather than being some fit of pique, this decision was astute of Korchnoi, not only for quality of life reasons but also because it ensured he would actually get to play the elite games for which his ability qualified him – if he stayed in the USSR, he never knew when the authorities might ban him from the board again. Thereafter, in swift succession, Korchnoi competed for the Dutch, then the West Germans, then the Swiss. At the time of the 1978 championship, he was actually considered 'stateless' – I couldn't think of another world championship in any sport or pursuit in which that has been the case, but to my surprise research shows that independent athletes compete at the Olympics relatively frequently.

Whilst the USSR predictably used all sorts of epithets about him, Korchnoi seemed to regard his newfound rootless status as a badge of honour. The proposal was vetoed by the authorities, but in pre-match negotiations about flags to be used for the qualifiers, Korchnoi's second, Britain's own Raymond Keene, proposed that he play under the skull and crossbones. Lad.

Russia tried to muscle the defector off the pitch, seeking to have him banned from the qualifying tournament. In that rare thing, an example of the sporting authorities being brave and getting the big call right, the Soviets were told to do one. Korchnoi won, gaining the right to face Karpov at last. And it was a decidedly odd affair.

For starters, Karpov had a hypnotist on his support team. Korchnoi had two locals who were, er, on bail for attempted murder. This is unconventional. (On the other hand, Karpov's 'ex'-KGB colonel acting as his minder can be regarded as entirely normal.) The chairs on which the players were to sit for the match were X-rayed before play, amidst talk of death rays having been installed. None were found.

The delivery of yoghurts to Karpov was the subject of wild allegations that their arrival constituted the passing of messages about the current state of play (whether to draw, how likely he was to win from this position and so forth) from his support team, perhaps conveyed by the timing of such delivery or the colour of the yoghurt. Or perhaps the flavour. But don't worry. After prolonged negotiation, it was agreed that yoghurt could still be served during play – if the colour was pre-agreed, the server was pre-identified and the timing of the delivery was pre-fixed. So that was the big issue taken care of.

Korchnoi also had a lady friend in tow who'd spent ten years being detained by the Russians after trumped-up charges of espionage in the Soviet-occupied zone of Vienna. It is right to say that she wasn't really a fan of the USSR, and she loudly and firmly expressed her political views throughout the championships with some regularity.

Several world championships had been played in an atmosphere of hatred. Alekhine and Capablanca, for example, could have been throwing knives rather than moving pieces. Whilst Fischer and Spassky didn't hate each other,[*] they represented superpowers that did.

But the animosity on show in Baguio was on another level. Korchnoi used the public platform offered by the world championship to air the (very understandable) grievances in his private life: urging the release of his wife and son (who were still in the USSR) in an open letter to the Soviets published prior to the match, he referred to Karpov as 'one of the jailers of my family'. Oof.

Spectators were hard to come by after the championship kicked off with a record seven drawn games. Before the eighth, Karpov refused to shake Korchnoi's hand as is customary, citing all the recent events as proof that goodwill was lacking anyway.

Always thin-skinned, the offended Korchnoi lost his

---

[*]   Indeed, they were lifelong friends.

temper and played angrily, and Karpov had the first win of the match at last. Korchnoi's play was referred to by Raymond Keene as 'consistent but suicidal' and Karpov's needling an opponent so effectively as 'immoral but astute'. Quite.

Post-yoghurtgate came hypnotistgate. Vladimir Zukhar was a famous hypnotist in the Karpov camp; the Korchnoi group complained about him sitting close to the front of the audience, staring intently at their man. The point is that whatever your views on hypnotism, such things can be off-putting when you're trying to concentrate. The adjudicators had a meeting about the issue. For six hours. Afterwards, Zukhar moved back, a bit. Korchnoi's lady friend took to kicking the hypnotist and stabbing him with a pen. (The hypnotism issue was later settled over drinks between the groups in the absence of the players and Korchnoi's LF: Zukhar would sit at the back as long as Korchnoi stopped wearing his reflective glasses designed to repel hypnotic rays.)

Complaints were now falling like rain from both sides. At the board, Korchnoi drew even, 1–1 (with nine draws), despite an academic writing from Cambridge to kindly let him know that distance hypnosis was indeed possible. Fog rolled into the rooms from a storm, briefly managing the impossible feat of temporarily stopping the arguments.

Suddenly, Karpov won two games on the bounce. In heavenly sympathy for Korchnoi, perhaps, there was a prompt earthquake and lightning struck the hotel. I know you think I'm making this up by now, but I'm not. A landslide behind the playing hall killed two people. Rain flooded out some of the hotel rooms. Play carried on.

The hotel generator exploded. No big fire, which was surely the first plus for a while, but the arena was plunged into darkness for a day. When they could next play, Korchnoi wasted a quarter of an hour on his clock threatening the hypnotist with physical violence if he didn't move further back in the hall. He lost. Karpov four; Korchnoi one.

The pair on bail for attempted murder now arrived. They were in Korchnoi's entourage courtesy of his LF and were enlisted from a devout religious sect in order to send positive prayerful messages to their contender. Whether such ministrations were unavailable from penitents not presently on bail remains unknown. Anyway, in successive restrictions they were coerced into civilian clothes rather than their colourful robes and turbans, out of the lotus position onto chairs in the conventional style and finally banished from the spectating area altogether by an agreement between the two supporting camps to exclude those with serious criminal convictions. They continued to give mental comfort and spiritual guidance to Korchnoi – seemingly productively. On the other hand, having to give evidence to a Baguio police department as they investigated a group of Filipinos threatening Korchnoi with physical violence if he did not pay them $15,000 in return for (unsolicited) black magic support distracted from things for a day or two.

One more win apiece: Karpov five; Korchnoi two – with twenty draws. Then a major Korchnoi comeback, with him winning three out of four games in a row. Karpov was in a minor car crash before the fourth Korchnoi win and got severely sunburnt before the fifth.

So things were level at 5–5; one more win for either player would decide things. Raymond Keene says that, at this point, the organisers suggested to his camp that things had gone on so long, and the players were so tired, the match should be cancelled and the championship begun again the next year, with results reset at 0–0.

CAN YOU IMAGINE COMING BACK TO DO ALL THIS AGAIN?

Understandably, given the run of form and the re-markable damp squib it would have made the tumultu-ous championship for those watching around the world, Keene declined without even telling his player of the offer, to avoid throwing him off his game.

But Korchnoi lost the next game.

So, after three months (yes, months) of play, Karpov beat Korchnoi six wins to five, with twenty-one draws. Korchnoi played at the highest level for the rest of his life but was never to become world champion. He would never come this close again. (I note that FIDE, the governing chess body, pulled the same 'cancel and start again' routine seven years later, protecting Karpov – still world champi-on – from the resurgent challenger Garry Kasparov, the cancellation coming off successfully this time.)

Korchnoi is remembered as one of the strongest players in the modern era never to have been world champion. All in all, he was a candidate ten times. He had a lifetime even score record with Fischer and beat the current world champion, Magnus Carlsen.

What of the controversy about Fischer walking away from the scene? Does it undermine Karpov's achievement? Well, not to me. Chess matches – like any form of competition – are won only by those prepared to compete.

What's the lesson we might take from this chess marathon? It seems invidious to say that sometimes an anticlimactic draw after all the emotion and slog is your best option after all. Avoiding spiritual guidance from those with murderous intentions seems trite, too. Perhaps it's that the more secondary disputes and distractions you pile up for yourself, the less likely your primary aim is to come off. This, if nothing else from the magnificently weird Baguio round of the World Chess Championships in 1978, seems a universal lesson.

*　　*　　*

There are two unpleasant codas to this story; in both of them, the full spite of the Soviet regime is on show.

Korchnoi's son was supposedly given an undertaking that he could follow his father into exile if he surrendered his passport to the authorities. So doing, he was promptly drafted into the Soviet Army, arrested and then charged when he didn't perform army service. He was sentenced to two and a half years in a labour camp and served his full sentence. In 1982, *six years* after Korchnoi's defection, he was finally allowed to leave the country.

Second, in the course of his journey to the 1972 championship, Fischer was the cause of one of my favourite and the saddest chess one-liners. In Vancouver in 1971, he crushed the Soviet grandmaster and concert pianist Mark Taimanov 6–0 in their quarter final in the candidates' tournament. Taimanov, whose chess career – a lifetime of hard work – was effectively ended by the USSR after the humiliation, said to him across the board, 'Well, I still have my music.' But such was the spite of the Russian authorities that, in fact, he didn't. Not only was he banned from playing chess thereafter – they banned him from the concert stage, too.

CHAPTER 26

THERE'S NO PLACE LIKE HOME

Thomas Pellow, from Cornwall, was eleven years old when he was serving, in the summer of 1715, as a cabin boy on a ship captained by his uncle. They had sailed across the Bay of Biscay and reached Cape Finisterre when they were captured by Barbary pirates. (Side note: these were perhaps the most successful pirates in history. Post-independence from Great Britain, threats to American shipping posed by the Barbary corsairs were directly responsible in part for the formation of the US Navy.)

So, Pellow became a slave of Sultan Moulay Ismail ibn Sharif. The Sultan was not known for his kindness. On one occasion, the story goes, he came with his army to a river where there was no convenient point at which to cross. Having prisoners with him, he ordered them killed and their bodies lashed together to fashion a bridge.

The Sultan gave Thomas to his son, Muley Spha, who promptly tortured him until he converted to Islam. This was a rather short-lived success for Muley Spha. The Sultan ordered that Thomas should be sent to learn Arabic, and when his son refused to obey said order, the Sultan had him killed on the spot. In front of Thomas.

So, when he was asked if he would like to become a

soldier for the Sultan, Pellow said… oh, yes, please. And, as it happens, he learned Arabic PDQ.

Pellow swiftly became a leading light in the Sultan's elite fighting corps of European slaves. Most, like him, had been seized as children and raised in an indoctrinated system. Pellow fought in three campaigns, often leading his fellow slaves into battle – and on one occasion leading a slave-capturing expedition himself.

He eventually escaped aboard a ship bound for Gibraltar. When he arrived there, he was initially barred from disembarking by the British authorities because he was taken to be a Barbary pirate. Which, in a sense, he was.

He had spent twenty-three years of his life in captivity in service to the Sultan. On his return home to Cornwall, he could not recognise his own parents – and, for their part, they only 'recognised' him as they had been told of his impending return. He was an alien in the land to which he had longed to return for two decades, and likely felt more at home in the land from which he had devoutly wished to flee.

The lesson to take from Thomas Pellow's story is a hard one. Home isn't always home. Harder still: sometimes, no matter how much we wish it to be different, there *is* no 'home'.

CHAPTER 27

THEY ALSO SERVE WHO ONLY STAND AND WAIT

As we saw with the tale of the Calcutta Light Horse, sometimes the brave are to be found in retirement – but ready to serve when the call comes. Wolraad Woltemade was a dairy farmer. He had been a soldier with the Dutch East India Company and settled at Cape Town in his pastoral semi-retirement. June is midwinter in the southern hemisphere, and during a gale in June 1773, the ship *De Jonge Thomas* was driven aground at the mouth of the Salt river, which feeds into Table Bay. (The word '*jonge*' makes me think of genever – a reaction likely to be common amongst those who like a drink and have been to Amsterdam.) The ship began to break up. Many aboard drowned, but many others clung perilously to the hull as it seesawed to and fro on a sandbar in the gale.

Things could hardly have been crueller if the conditions had been deliberately designed to give false hope. The ship was not far from shore – but the water was icy, the cross-current from the river mouth was strong and almost all who attempted to swim the seemingly short distance to safety were drowned.

As the situation became more desperate, a crowd

gathered upon the shore. Some in sympathy, some in hope of flotsam and jetsam – none to actually do anything to aid those in increasing peril. Until Woltemade arrived.

He was only there because he had come to give some food to his son, one of the soldiers sent to keep order on the beach – not to help but to maintain law and order on the shore as the crowd continued to grow. Woltemade, and Woltemade alone, was spurred by his conscience to act. He rode out towards the sandbank on his horse. His mount swam powerfully to the ship's side. Calling out to those upon the wreck, Woltemade told two men to leap into the water and hold the horse's tail. They did. He turned and pulled them into shore. Then turned and rode back out.

Seven times he did this successfully. As he and his exhausted horse rested, the wreck began to collapse completely. Immediately, he rode out once more. But seeing their last chance for safety, not two but six men leapt. Their weight dragged the horse under, along with Woltemade. All were drowned.

Some 191 people were aboard the *Jonge Thomas*. Only fifty-three survived the disaster; fourteen had been rescued by Woltemade.

Many things in South Africa were named after our hero, including a medal, but my favourite is a tugboat. The perfect namesake. The lesson from the wreck of the *Jonge Thomas* and the lives lost amongst the souls who sailed in her is simple but hard – and harder still for those who actually find themselves in situations in which it becomes relevant: sometimes, not all can be saved. Sometimes, not only can the salvation of all concerned be impossible, but if this lesson is not understood, the gallant and brave will also be dragged to their deaths by those they seek to rescue. Sometimes you have to wait. Even if death is waiting too. This is why there is great dignity in the sacrifice and stoicism contained in the simple, enduring line, 'Women and children first.' That is, if we are still allowed to use such terms today.

CHAPTER 28

ADVICE IS SELDOM TRULY FREE

Bob Boothby was an astute observer of and player in British politics. He was one of the few Churchill loyalists in the wilderness years between the wars, and he benefited from that loyalty in his subsequent advancement in the Conservative Party, in government and eventually to the Lords. (Albeit in terms of senior offices held he considerably foreshortened his own horizons as he preferred performing in the TV studio to working in a ministry.)

Anyway, he was parliamentary private secretary (PPS) to Churchill when he was Chancellor in the 1920s – a 'sterile' time for Churchill, in Boothby's view, which seems right. Despite his no doubt onerous duties at No. 11, Churchill was busily churning out *The World Crisis*, his six-volume account of the First World War.

One day, Churchill summoned his PPS, because, as Boothby tells us (the classically brazen namedropper often putting the declaration of his *extremely* good connections in the quotes of others in his memoirs), he knew Boothby to be 'a great friend of Lloyd George'. Churchill asked Boothby to fix up a meeting with Lloyd George to fill in some points on the Great War for the book for him. This, Boothby did. Churchill and Lloyd George had an hour together in private in No. 11. After Lloyd George had left,

Boothby headed in to see his boss. The meeting had gone well, it seemed. But then, 'A hard look came into his face … "Within five minutes the old relationship between us was completely re-established. The relationship between Master and Servant. And I was the Servant."'

Quite a thing for *that* ego to have been able to concede, isn't it?

The lesson from this brief but insightful anecdote about our greatest Prime Minister is a useful one: advice is seldom truly free.

Postscript. Boothby was one of many prominent Brits in Germany during the 1930s and one of the few who emerge with much credit. On the receiving end of a 'Heil Hitler' complete with salute, he famously returned the gesture with a cheery 'Heil Boothby!'

Second postscript. Despite much legal action to keep things out of the papers at the time, it eventually emerged that Boothby was on intimate social terms with the Kray twins. It may not surprise you to know that these are names he *doesn't* drop in his memoirs.

CHAPTER 29

RUB FOR LUCK

Most Brits, if they know it at all, think of and dismiss Bergamo as a hub for low-cost airlines; a place to endure and dash away from. Or, latterly, as a Covid hotspot.

This is a mistake. Because it's a magnificent Italian hill town with a fantastic old Città Alta of beautiful buildings, breathtaking views, a funicular,* cafés older than countries, sixteenth-century walled defences and some interesting history to go with it. But this is not a tourism guide. It's a story about testicles.

In the time of the Condottieri – captains of mercenary companies, who became powerful social and political figures in their own rights – one captain who rose to prominence was Bartolomeo Colleoni.

The Colleonis were a prominent Bergamo family. Bartolomeo, modest fellow, wanted to build a chapel to his own glory, but the spot he rather fancied for it was already occupied by the sacristy of an existing church. So, his soldiers pulled that down.

The Colleoni chapel built in its place, finished in 1476, is the result. It's a stunning piece of marbled architecture, with the Colleoni symbol prominently displayed on the

---

* No British person can read this word without humming the tune you are humming to yourself now.

tomb and the exterior gates. The symbol is three slightly stylised testicles. Because Bartolomeo Colleoni was blessed with a third. Quite the coincidence given that his family name means testicles. Rather than feeling any shyness about it, he embraced his unusual condition, putting it on his shield, his coat of arms and so forth. Presumably, his men fought under it.

Colleoni frequently switched sides between the Venetians and the Milanese; his versatility ensured that he never went without soldierly work. He even became the Captain General of Venice, the foremost military gig of his day and, to the English ear at least, a peculiar and rather nice title.* (Failure by the Venetians to award him this title previously led to one of his switches of loyalty to Milan, so it might be fair to say that he forced them into it.) By the time of his death, he had amassed a huge amount of cash, and he left behind a fantastic architectural legacy that survives to this day.

So it seems that he enjoyed great good fortune. As Bergamo's alpha male, he certainly had much virility and strength: perhaps, too, he benefited from greater than usual amounts of testosterone. Certainly, the legend that grew up around him (and was encouraged by him) suggested such conclusions.† (He was certainly more fortunate than

---

* The title is not unknown in the UK. It is held by the Royal Patron of the Royal Marines – which was, when I started writing this book, Prince Harry, and is now not.

† This condition is a plot device in J. P. Donleavy's mildly amusing novel *The Onion Eaters*; the protagonist, who has it, is widely admired and envied for his apparently familial trait. The extent to which Donleavy was indebted to Colleoni remains unknown.

his father, Paolo, who, after an illustrious military career in his own right, was assassinated by his cousins.)

Visitors to Bergamo appear to believe in this good fortune too: whilst the rest of the metalwork on the heavy gates to the chapel is a dull dark brown, the gonads are burnished to a brassy light golden sheen by all the vigorous rubbing for luck. I hesitate even to attempt to draw a lesson to be learned from this story.

CHAPTER 30

THE SILENT AND UNSEEN

My grandfather was a glider pilot at Arnhem, so I have always taken an interest in paratroopers. The first Allied parachute drop in enemy territory was Operation Colossus, in early 1941 – it was a raid carried out in Italy by British commandos in a unit that became part of the SAS. It was a very mixed bag: whilst it successfully tested the concept that such missions could be done, the aqueduct they targeted was swiftly repaired and they were all caught by the Italians. Just one week later, though, there was a much more significant raid – the first of many by the unit concerned and by the Special Operations Executive – and this one was not carried out by the British.

The Cichociemni (chick-a-chem-ney) were Polish paratroopers. Cichociemni means 'the silent and unseen'. They trained in exile at Audley End, a beautiful stately home in Essex, perhaps best known to you because a nearby railway station is named after it. Our heroes generally trained in secret in Audley End's grounds, but they did conduct some forays further afield in the local area. One involved doing a mock raid on the train station – so you can spare them a thought the next time you pass through it on the way to Cambridge.

They also did a full-blown attack exercise on the local

post office, which was no doubt a treat for Mrs Goggins. Night manoeuvres led to punch-ups with both Essex Police and Home Guard units, who were presumably surprised by these lads charging around their patch. Joined-up bureaucracy fails again.

Naturally, their historic first drop was a raid behind enemy lines in their beloved Polish homeland, which was of course occupied by the Germans, on 15–16 February 1941. Three agents were returned to Poland after a five-and-a-half-hour flight from RAF Stradishall, a little to the south of my native Bury St Edmunds in Suffolk.* It wasn't an ideal first attempt: they were dropped 30 miles from the intended drop site. Still, Arkady Rzegocki, the Polish ambassador to the UK, said that the Chicochemni's first mission offered a 'glimmer of hope to the besieged homeland that help was coming'.

Over the years, the Cichociemni delivered funds and materiel to the resistance, became officers in the Polish Secret Army and taught others the guerrilla warfare techniques they had learned. They also conveyed agents to be embedded in the underground movement. The Cichociemni were all volunteers. Britain is proud to have trained them in covert operations, cryptography, intelligence-gathering, sabotage and queueing. Some 316 Cichociemni were dropped into occupied Poland between 1941 and 1945; 103 died in combat or were executed after

---

* The base closed in 1970 and the site is now occupied by two prisons. Highpoint North was briefly a women's prison and was the final prison that incarcerated Myra Hindley before her death. After it reverted to being a men's prison, Boy George was an inmate. For its part, Highpoint South has had Tony Martin and George Michael as inmates.

being captured by the Germans. Eighteen more died in action in the Warsaw Uprising.

Their raids were stopped in 1944 after most of Poland was occupied by the Red Army. A grim indication of the future that awaited their country is given by the fact that in addition to those killed by Nazis, nine further Cicho-ciemni were executed after the war by the Polish communist regime.

Some 527 Poles completed their special training at Audley End House. Heroes all. Did you know that this sedate spot in Essex was (in the words of English Heritage) 'the spiritual home of wartime resistance' for the Poles?

You do now.

CHAPTER 31

I'VE GOT TO BE ME

Adeline, Countess of Cardigan and Lancastre (not a typo), played fast and loose with naming conventions – a habit which may have stemmed from her father's use in later life of his mother's cool maiden name, 'de Horsey',* to make him Spencer Horsey de Horsey. Which is nicer than the apian cruelty of his own name, Kilderbee.

Briefly engaged to a pretender to the Spanish throne, Adeline scandalised society by being seen out and about with a friend of her father's, the notorious rake the 7th Earl of Cardigan (who was separated from his wife), without a chaperone – *quelle horreur*! After the no doubt much lamented death of the Earl's wife, they formalised things by getting married themselves.

They tied the knot in Gibraltar, momentarily away from the censorious eyes of the court and the press, for she vacillated between flirting with public attention and ostentatiously shunning it. This doesn't remind us of anyone in the present day, of course.

Her first husband gets one of the best lines in the history of cinema: played by Trevor Howard, upon being given the order (or not; the question is disputed) to carry out the

---

* The Horseys were, of course, from Bury St Edmunds.

94

Charge of the Light Brigade, Lord Cardigan announces: 'Well, here goes the last of the Brudenells. The brigade will advance!'*

Adeline received numerous proposals after Cardigan's death in 1868. One came from her lifelong acquaintance Benjamin Disraeli, who wasn't badly placed in terms of the kind of eye-catching public role she liked, as he was then in post for his first short stint as Prime Minister. She was certainly fond of Disraeli, but marriage was out of the question given his halitosis. So, she married a Portuguese nobleman, Don António Manuel de Saldanha e Lancastre, Conde de Lancastre, in 1873. It was by whacking the two titles together, which apparently was a no-no,[†] that she got the moniker that graces her rather racy memoirs.

After some time together in Lisbon and Paris, she parted ways with Don Longname, whose bronchitis meant he avoided English weather, and returned to live at the home left to her by Cardigan. She remained on good terms with her husband, visiting him from time to time, but their separation was for good. Did she revert to Britain for some quiet in her twilight years? Oh, no. It is fair to say that she did not go gentle into that good night.

---

[*] Film has been rather kinder to Cardigan than historians, who have exhaustively explored the extent to which he was a very poor officer, derelict in almost every duty. Whilst undoubtedly possessed of significant personal courage, it seems that both competence and even interest in carrying out the responsibilities of the high military offices he actively sought evaded him.

[†] An alternative offered for the strong and seemingly court-inspired contemporary resentment of her amalgamated title is the fact that Queen Victoria used the title 'Countess of Lancaster' when travelling on the Continent incognito. (I mean, plainly it can't really be incognito if you're travelling as a Countess and are as beachball-esquely recognisable as Victoria, but the point stands.)

Her pursuits scandalised society in ways we might find surprising. She rode a bicycle – modern interpretation straight to sainthood; Victorian interpretation unladylike. She smoked – modern interpretation straight to hell; Victorian interpretation pearl-clutching; interpretation in between more sympathetic. In her seventies, she would entertain guests by running steeplechases through the estate's graveyard, or by playing the castanets in full dancing regalia, or by dressing up as a ghost haunting her own house. A nun, in fact. She had a sense of humour. These activities were interrupted only slightly by her bankruptcy.

Her approach to death was equally eccentric. In her twilight years, she took to keeping a coffin in her ballroom and would regularly get in it when visitors came calling, to ask them how they thought she looked. She remained married to the Don until his death and survived him by quite some time. She died at Deene (no relation) Park in Northamptonshire and is buried there with Cardigan.

What lesson might one draw from the life and adventures of Adeline? Well, I haven't seen her grave, but I would not be at all surprised if it had a lengthy cod Latin motto which roughly translated means, 'I did what I liked – so what?' Possibly atop a rococo stylised V-sign. Be yourself, no matter what they say. Unless what they say amuses you, in which case, good.

CHAPTER 32

LIFE AS A HIGHWIRE ACT

Ignaz Trebitsch-Lincoln was born to an Orthodox Jewish family in Hungary. It was the last orthodox thing he ever did. Whilst he did not complete his studies at the Royal Hungarian Academy of Dramatic Art, I think you'll agree that what follows confirms a flair for the extraordinary.

Regularly arrested for theft, he abandoned his course of studies and moved to England, where he converted to Christianity. He was sent to Germany by missionaries to train for religious orders – a vocation for which subsequent events showed him to be singularly ill-suited.

He was tasked by the church with converting Jews in Canada to Christianity but soon returned to the UK as he was unhappy about his pay. He charmed the Archbishop of Canterbury into giving him a curacy, as one does. Plainly he had a gift for acquiring mentors and convincing them to assist his advancement.

Soon after, he came to meet Seebohm Rowntree, the millionaire confectioner, becoming his private secretary and thenceforth the Liberal Party's candidate for the Darlington constituency, as Rowntree was a luminary of the Liberals. He was successfully elected to Parliament at the general election of January 1910. (He'd only become a

British citizen in mid-1909 – after he'd been selected as a candidate!)

But 1910 saw two general elections, and Trebitsch-Lincoln didn't stand in the second in November. At that time, MPs were unpaid – his finances had not improved since his election and he couldn't afford to run again. A series of failed business ventures took up his time before the war. When conflict loomed, naturally our man felt the call to serve.

Not in the front line, of course. He rather thought of himself as a spy, actually. And when his adopted country turned down his services, he did the obvious thing: he offered himself to the Germans. They said yes please, and he became a double agent, having rather failed to be a single agent.

The Brits were on to him quite promptly, as whatever else his failings he was an *éminence grise* in the all mouth and no trousers championships and made poor to no effort in covering his tracks as he talked up the important spying work he hadn't actually done. He fled to the USA.

In the States, the German Embassy had received orders not to touch this lunatic, which is understandable. So, he sold his story. The MP who became a spy. It was a sensation. The UK's extradition treaty with the USA didn't cover spying, so he was sent back on a fraud charge, which seems right. The Americans sent him back and the Brits put him to work in the post office as he awaited his trial. After a shift one evening, he treated his guards to a round in the pub, legged it out the pub window and made his way back to the USA, where he was deported back to us again.

He did three years in prison* and was eventually deported with his British citizenship revoked. On the Continent, he wormed his way into the nascent Nazi regime, writing for newspapers opposed to the post-First World War settlement at Versailles. He was sent to interview the Dutch Crown Prince, who refused to see him. Details, details; he came back from Amsterdam full of news about how well his interview had gone.

As a well-known arbiter of truth, he became the press censor for the new post-Kapp Putsch German 'government', which briefly seized power from the Weimar regime in 1920. When that fell, he tried various other fringe political movements. One, the White International (a clutch of Hungarian and Russian fascists), made him their archivist. 'Me? Ignaz Trebitsch-Lincoln? Given your secrets? With *my* reputation?' He promptly sold them to every country buying.

He was deported from Austria. He went to the USA again but was… asked to leave. Trebitsch-Lincoln was fast running out of countries. So, he went to China, where he worked for a warlord called General Yang Sen and converted to Buddhism.

(Digression: Trebitsch-Lincoln had a son who joined the British Army. Said son burgled a man and shot him dead. He was sentenced to death in a military court, as

---

* At HMP Parkhurst on the Isle of Wight. Now it's not a high-security establishment, but then it was one of the UK's toughest prisons.

he was a soldier at the time of his offence. His father couldn't get back to the UK in time to see him before his execution.)

In China, Trebitsch-Lincoln established a new monastery, of which he was the abbot. It attracted some European initiates, so it was rather more successful than his Christian conversion work in Canada. New monks would have to give their possessions… to the abbot. He seduced a lot of nuns.

There's only so long a man can stay on the straight and narrow, and before long he changed his loyalties again, writing anti-British material for Japan. His Nazi tendencies re-emerged upon the outbreak of the Second World War, as he offered to organise Buddhists for the Germans in an anti-British effort. The price for his invaluable work – in addition to hard cash, obviously – was a face-to-face meeting with the Führer, at which he promised to conjure up various Buddhist spirits. It may very well seem to you to be something that anyone would dismiss out of hand, but the Nazis were well known for their credulous fondness for mystical schemes, and Himmler and Hess were both keen on this wheeze. But the wheels fell off when Hess made his solo flight to Scotland in 1941 – one of the maddest stories ever told and rather better known than this one.

So, Trebitsch-Lincoln had to content himself with declaring himself the Dalai Lama – a claim that Japan actually supported – when the 13th Dalai Lama and the Panchen Lama had both died without replacements in a short period of time. How his putative global spiritual leadership would have fared is a question to which sadly we will never know the answer. For, in a moment of decency, Ignaz Trebitsch-Lincoln wrote a letter of protest to Adolf Hitler about the Holocaust. The Nazis asked their Japanese allies to arrest him, which they did, and, allegedly, to poison him. Whether they did or not, he promptly died, in 1943, of a stomach ailment.

CHAPTER 33

HIGH SCORE

This one is about sport, and I promise that you don't have to like sport to enjoy it. This is the story of a highest ever score; a score that will never, ever be beaten. It is the story of Maurice Flitcroft.

Maurice had been an ice cream man. A shoe polish salesman. A gofer on a building site. A crane operator. But with all due respect to these roles, they were the warm-up to his crowning achievement: his appearance in the qualifiers for the 1976 Open, the holiest of all golfing holies.

Don't get me wrong. It's not that he had never played. He'd had a go in a field and on a beach. And he'd read a couple of articles. He even had half a set of clubs, which is half a set more than me. But his decision to enter himself as a professional in the ultimate golf tournament was going some.

Amateurs had to have an established handicap but professionals – until the Maurice Flitcroft rule was applied straight after the 1976 Open – did not. So, he simply called himself a professional.

He was in. Remarkably, nobody seemed to notice that they'd never heard of him before. And once he was in, he was in. He played the whole course with his half-bag of mail-order clubs. He went round... in 121. This is not a good golf score. It is, in fact, forty-nine over par. It is the worst score in the history of the Open, by miles. What a lad.

His fellow professionals did not see the funny side. In fact, many of them went bananas. Did they not realise that this was the first time that a good slice of the public had taken any interest in their game – and had a new hero in it? (Plus, what does the word 'Open' mean to you, anyway?)

In a similarly grumpy vein, event organisers the R&A banned him for life. Which seems a bit harsh. He could only improve from that round, after all – how were they to know that this was not the start of a magnificent career? They also put in place new rules to ensure that 'professional' actually means 'professional'. Thus we can say with certainty that Maurice's achievement shall be graven in tablets of stone for all time. The highest ever score, for ever more.

The 1976 Open was graced by many first-class golfers. A nineteen-year-old Seve Ballesteros hit the scene.[*] Many fine strokes were played. But for many – nay, for most – it is remembered for one thing: a chain-smoking crane operator from Barrow-in-Furness with chutzpah by the lorryload.[†]

Maurice's memoirs remain tragically unpublished (they include the gem of a claim that he would have done a lot

---

[*] Indeed, there is a wonderful black-and-white photograph of a bemused-looking young Seve walking in tandem with Flitcroft, which you can find online.

[†] Let me prove that. The Open that year was won by Johnny Miller. Did you know that? Of course you didn't. With no disrespect meant to Mr Miller.

better if he hadn't left his best club in the car), but, Covid allowing, the long-awaited movie, with Mark Rylance starring as Maurice, is due for release in 2021. If we still have cinemas. I'll watch it.

CHAPTER 34

THE RISE AND FALL OF A RAIDER

Admiral Maximilian von Spee was a good sailor who died in the First World War during the destruction of the East Asia Fleet he commanded,[*] along with both of his sons and circa 2,000 other Germans, at the hands of the British at the Battle of the Falkland Islands.[†] Before that fateful battle took place, and indeed even before the Battle of Coronel prior to it, in which he gave us a pasting, Spee did something interesting.

He feared – rightly – that the time would come when he would be outnumbered and outgunned by a combined Allied fleet. At that point, his armoured cruisers would either prevail or they wouldn't. The presence of the ancillary, less powerful ships in the squadron would make little difference to the outcome of the battle and might well entail their destruction. His Pacific Squadron included a light cruiser called the *Emden*. She was commanded by Karl von Müller, an extremely capable man. In the

---

[*] After von Spee's death, a number of vessels were named after him, including the famous 'pocket battleship' the *Admiral Graf Spee*, sunk at the Battle of the River Plate in the Second World War.

[†] This was one of many naval battles of the nineteenth and twentieth centuries which saw extremely lopsided results. The number of German casualties is debated but is somewhere around 2,200. The British casualty list is clear: ten fatalities.

thinking of the day, the *Emden*'s armament wasn't powerful enough to play a part in a battle squadron. But she was fast, managing over 24 knots; she was well armed for her class; and she could cover over 6,000 nautical miles in a single cruise. In short, she was born to raid. So, at Müller's suggestion, Spee cut the *Emden* loose.

When the squadron was put to sea from the Mariana Islands, the fleet went one way; the *Emden* went another. She was henceforth a free agent, released to sail and raid alone.* OK, not quite alone as they had a supply ship sailing with them, but it sounded more dramatic the way I put it. (The *Emden*'s supply ship was called the *Markomannia*, which was no doubt a perfectly good vessel, but to my ear the name sounds like a pre-Euro German gameshow.)

It took them four weeks to sail to the Indian Ocean. They made good use of the time. The crew of the *Emden* were not only gifted with speed, range and firepower; they were also blessed with guile. Their ship (which was coal-powered) had three funnels. On their voyage they fitted a fake fourth funnel. This was an extremely good wheeze. It disguised her lines, giving her an outline on the horizon similar to the Yarmouth class of *British* cruisers.

---

* Müller and the *Emden* had already shown their capabilities in this field; on their way to the Mariana Islands rendezvous with the Pacific Squadron, Müller had captured the *Rjesan* (or *Ryazan*), a Russian ship. Whilst perhaps a modest prize – it was a mail steamer – it was nevertheless the first taken in the war by the Imperial German Navy. The *Rjesan* was refitted as a raider herself but was such an abject failure that she was put in at Guam to be interned for the rest of the war by the Americans. A pretty ignominious fate for a ship, even if undoubtedly a rather nice one for her crew.

It might, they thought, let them get closer to their prey before the threat they posed was appreciated.

It worked a charm. Her successes began on 10 September when the Greek cargo ship *Pontoporos* was captured – an ideal prize as, in addition to equipment bound for the British, thus denying the enemy useful materiel, she was also carrying coal, giving a new lease of life to the time the *Emden* could stay at sea a-raiding before having to put to shore for refuelling.

The next day, the *Indus*, a transport ship full of British troops, was stopped and sunk after the men had been transferred to the *Pontoporos*. The next, the *Kabinga*, was a cargo ship, which Müller released to sail back to Calcutta with the crews of his first two captures aboard. The legend of the *Emden* began to spread.

The very next day, the *Emden* claimed two more victims, the *Killin* and the *Diplomat*, a 7,600-tonner loaded with tea. The accumulated tonnage of vessels sunk by this single ship started to soar. The day after, another two – the *Clan Matthews*, full of agricultural and rail goods, and the *Trabbock*.

Panic spread amongst those responsible for the safety of British shipping – and amongst the seamen. Australia delayed the dispatch of troopships bound for Britain and the war. After only a week, the *Emden*'s effect had begun to bite, with serious results for the Allies.

Müller, after stopping the Italian ship *Loredano* but allowing her to proceed with her voyage (no doubt burnishing the fast-growing story of the *Emden* amongst the sailors of the Indian Ocean), decided to make for fresh hunting ground. The *Emden* appeared off the coast of Madras on the night of 22 September. At a range of 3,000 yards, choosing a line of fire designed to minimise harm to civilians in the city, she shelled the storage tanks of the Burmah Oil Company. Up went 1,000 tons of fuel. I'm trying to imagine what a fire that big looks like.

It's worth noting that efforts to stop the *Emden* at this point were somewhere between ineffectual and positively harmful. At Madras, the shore battery blazed away at her to zero effect. The next night, off Colombo, searchlights seeking her out were helpful to Müller in sinking a big merchant ship full of sugar – after taking her crew off and putting them aboard the *Markomannia*.

Two more days, four more victims, one of which was carrying coal, and it was time to disappear and pop up elsewhere, as by this point some sixteen warships – British, French, Japanese, Russian – were hunting the hunter. Finding ships at sea is surprisingly hard. Indeed, the Allies only knew the whereabouts of von Spee's large squadron when they revealed it by shelling Papeete.

The *Emden* could pick up how much wireless traffic there was in the area, so Müller had a good sense from the increased chatter that there were now many ships pursuing him. He headed south to Diego Garcia. Then, the island's only contact with the rest of the world was a twice-yearly visit by a steamer from Mauritius, the last having taken place prior to the outbreak of war, so the poor islanders were in the dark and positively welcomed his visit. He beached to have his keel scraped, with grateful thanks.

Revenge of sorts was taken whilst he was out of action. The *Yarmouth* – the poor maligned British cruiser whose lines he had aped – found and sank the *Markomannia* and recaptured the *Pontoporos*. The *Emden* was truly on her own now.

Solitude, it turns out, rather suited the *Emden*. In the shipping lanes at Cape Comorin, at the southern point of India, in the course of a few hours on 20 October she sank five British ships, stopped a sixth and put the crews from the other five aboard her, and captured a seventh. This was going some. Over 26,000 tons of Allied shipping had now been lost to the *Emden*. There had been sneaking admiration for the *Emden* and her exploits, especially given Müller's chivalrous behaviour with regard to crews, but up with this we would not put.

Harrumphing editorials in *The Times* called for an end to the reign of the *Emden*. The fact that millions of pounds and thousands of tons of goods had been lost was highlighted. Moreover, the fact that merchant shipping in a very wide area had been reduced to all but zero traffic mattered for the future of the war. As if to emphasise the accuracy of the increasingly alarmed noises in the Admiralty, the *Emden* promptly outdid herself. She brazenly sailed right into the bay at George Town, Penang, and torpedoed the Russian cruiser *Jemstchoug*, which broke in two and sank in under a minute.

Yet again, everyone had taken the *Emden* for the *Yarmouth*. You'd have thought that the Allies might have cottoned on by now. But the French destroyer *Mousquet* was signalling a hello to her false friend at George Town moments before she too was sunk. To her credit, her guns were firing as she went down by the bows.

Half the Indian Ocean was now covered in ships hunting the *Emden*. Even so, Müller stopped the British cargo ship *Newburn*, whose crew must have been terrified of the famous raider – only to put the survivors of the *Mousquet* aboard her and send her on her way. But the *Emden*'s luck was running out. Müller made for the Cocos Islands. His fourth funnel was up, but it was so battered by now that the shore watch saw the raider for what it was. Their SOS call got out before Müller could jam it.

By this time the Australian troop movements were back underway, so the signal for help was picked up by the cruisers guarding them – the *Melbourne*, the *Sydney* and the Japanese ship the *Ibuki*. Each was more powerful than the *Emden*. To the envy of her peers, the *Sydney* was dispatched from the convoy to deal with the *Emden* at last.

It was Müller's turn to be taken by surprise. He had sent a detachment of fifty men under his executive officer, the unfortunately named Hellmuth von Mücke, to blow up the radio station and related infrastructure on the island. He had to leave them there when the *Sydney* appeared on the horizon, nearing fast. The *Sydney* kept over 10,000 yards away and began firing. This was comfortably within range for the Australians but at the very outer limit for Müller's guns. The *Sydney* was faster, too, so attempts to narrow the gap, to outmanoeuvre or to flee were all un-likely to succeed. It is therefore greatly to the *Emden*'s credit that she struck first, destroying a turret and injuring a few of the *Sydney*'s crew. But this was the last damage done by the great raider *Emden*. Soon, Müller's ship was ablaze, his steering impaired by damage to his helm, his gun turrets and funnels destroyed.

Still firing with whatever he had left, putting off so much smoke the Australians thought she'd gone down, Müller ran his ship aground. The *Emden* was going no-where, so the *Sydney* simply left her there and turned to dispatch another German ship, the *Buresk*. This was a rather withering putdown.

The *Sydney* returned to the *Emden* hours later and asked by signal whether Müller wished to surrender (his colours were still aloft). Müller replied by Morse that he didn't understand what the *Sydney* had sent. The *Sydney* clarified by shelling them again.

Müller was thoroughly run aground. Some 115 of his crew were dead; fifty-six more were badly wounded. He'd started the fight fifty hands short because of the shore party. Not a gun on the ship could still be fired; Müller surrendered. Thus ended the glorious, gallant run of the SMS *Emden*.

Thus, too, ended the fight for Müller, the closest Germany has ever come to a bold buccaneer, yo ho. He was taken to Malta and then to England as a prisoner of war. He was physically weak as he had malaria but still tunnelled out of captivity only to be recaptured. After the war, he received his country's highest military honours, declined all suggestions that he should tell his story for profit, successfully ran for political office and, alas, soon succumbed to illness, dying in 1923.

But the crew of the *Emden* had a little more to add to the history books. Remember Mücke and co., left on Direction Island in the Cocos Islands? We can imagine their feelings as they witnessed the ending of their beloved ship out at sea, unable to help their crewmates, and them now left stranded on the island. The Australians knew they were there and were after them, but the Germans were full of enterprise like their skipper. They seized a schooner in the harbour, filled her with provisions and slipped past the *Sydney* under cover of darkness. They reached Sumatra, where the Dutch refused them permission to land, but Mücke arranged for the *Choising*, a German cargo ship berthed in the harbour, to meet him at sea. He and his remnant crew boarded it, evaded British patrols and were put ashore at Hodeidah in the Yemen.

To Germany's ally Turkey they made their way over land to return to the fight, crossing half the world to get back to it. They lost three men on the way in a pitched battle with Bedouins. By journey's end they had covered over 11,000km, making it one of the longest escapes known to history. Their determination and the success of their adventure on land is a fitting tribute and ending to the tale of Germany's famous raider.

CHAPTER 35

THE WHITE MOUSE

Kiwi-born and Australia-bred Nancy Wake was a free spirit from the word go. When she was sixteen, she ran away from home in Sydney to work as a nurse, then went to London to train as a journalist. She worked as a foreign correspondent in Paris and Vienna, seeing the rise of the Nazis at first hand.

When the war broke out, she was living in Marseille. She worked as an ambulance driver until France fell, when she joined the Resistance. Her work was known to the Gestapo, but her skilfulness in avoiding them was second to none – thus, they christened this mysterious operative 'The White Mouse'.

Things became harder once the Wehrmacht occupied Vichy France. Wake's network was betrayed. She escaped France into Spain; her husband, also part of the network, remained and was killed. Reaching the UK, she joined the Special Operations Executive (SOE), and after training she parachuted into Auvergne. Caught up in a tree in her descent, she was found dangling from its branches by the Resistance. Apocryphally or not, their leader is said to have told her he hoped all French trees would bring forth such beautiful fruit. She replied, entirely understandably, 'Don't give me that French shit.'

The SOE supplied weaponry and cash for distribution by Wake and her group, and she co-ordinated targets for attack in the run-up to D-Day. But keen to show their ability to defeat the Germans themselves, the Resistance overreached. They moved from guerrilla fighting to full combat in which they were outnumbered and outgunned. Wake proved herself every bit the equal of her male colleagues in heavy fighting and then in a retreat that took three days. With her group needing to tell London what was happening, she volunteered to cycle a 300-mile round trip to the nearest known SOE radio facility, doing so successfully. In times of relaxation, she also proved herself more than the equal of her comrades by drinking them under the table.

Joined by some Americans, Wake's group undertook several assaults on German vehicles and successfully defended themselves from an attack whilst continuing their distribution of materiel obtained from air drops. During one of the raids, she killed a German with her bare hands.

Wake's story is not without controversy. There were three women in their camp; companions of the men. They were being abused by them. Two, she convinced her comrades to release. The third, she interrogated and concluded was a spy. She ordered the Resistance to shoot her. They did.

Wake's group took part in further tough operations against the Germans, who were now on the back foot after the Allied invasion of southern France. Many fell around her – but Wake survived.

After the war, she remarried (an RAF bomber pilot) and ran unsuccessfully for political office in Australia several times. She returned to London after the death of her second husband and was to be found on her regular barstool at the Stafford Hotel belting down G&Ts and setting the world to rights into her nineties.

She died just shy of her ninety-ninth birthday. Her ashes were scattered over the hills upon which she had fought for freedom.

CHAPTER 36

A GÖRING

A Göring is our subject today. Not Hermann, the Nazi Göring, but his younger brother Albert, the anti-Nazi Göring. The Görings were a well-established family, but they lacked cash. They lived in a couple of fine properties with Albert and Hermann's godfather, who was, as it happens, of Jewish descent. Said godfather definitely had an affair with their mother before Albert was born, and Albert may or may not have been his son. (Albert's daughter claims her father told her that this was the case, but the dates don't quite work given time spent in different countries by the parties concerned. Perhaps he just devoutly wished it.)

Albert served his country in the First World War in the trenches, as his brother served her in the air. Between the wars, Albert sought an inoffensive life in engineering and the arts in Vienna. But of course, peace was not to be found for almost anyone in that post-Versailles world, and the Anschluss came for Austria.

From the beginning, Albert had no truck with Nazism. As the persecution of the Jews increased, so did his resistance to it. One anecdote I particularly like: one day, some Jewish women forced by the Nazis to clean the street were no doubt surprised to find a distinguished-looking chap kneel beside them to lend a hand. Outraged, the officer in charge of the detail demanded this oddball's identification papers – upon seeing the name Göring, rather than risk controversy with this illustrious family, he cancelled the whole thing as a bad job.

More substantively, Albert helped Jews to escape Germany. Definitely, not possibly. One such was his former boss in the film industry, Oskar Pilzer, and his family, who attest to this rescue (they resettled in the United States). He even forged his brother's signature on papers to help opponents of the regime get away.

Family is a funny thing. No doubt the behaviour of his brother was a source of ire for Hermann Göring – but the brothers were and remained close, and he protected Albert. Moreover, whilst he obviously didn't initiate any of them, Hermann actually helped Albert in some of his undertakings once they were underway, even as he went about orchestrating the persecution of the Jews at the highest level.

This is perhaps the best thing that can ever be said or written about Göring major, in his Nazi period at least. In the First World War, the elder Göring was a brave man who served his country well. What that young fighter ace would make of the hate-filled blimp he became is a very good question.

Anyway, Albert was not alone in his endeavours. He was in touch with the Czech resistance as he became the export director of the Škoda factory, and he helped them as best he could – even to the extent of sabotage at his own works, as the Czech workers attested after the war. He wasn't particularly subtle in all this. The Gestapo files show him to have been known as an enemy of the Reich. His anti-Nazi remarks were recorded and reported. His passport was seized by the authorities. An order was made to have him arrested – and even shot. But whenever he was caught, his brother would get him released.

In an industrialist ploy reminiscent of *Schindler's List*, Albert didn't just help the Jews who happened to be around him: he used his business ventures to actively find and release more. He sent for workers from the concentration camps and promptly released them somewhere safe.

After the war, the younger Göring spent over a year in Allied custody and was questioned during the Nuremberg trials, but he was, quite properly, swiftly released as his story of assisting Jews and others was verified by evidence given to his interrogators. Nuremberg was the last time he saw his brother.

He was tried once again in Czechoslovakia over allegations of Nazi activities in his time at the Škoda factory; the former workers gave masses of evidence on his behalf, and he was vindicated once again.

For all that this has been verified and demonstrated, Albert Göring struggled after the war. He never really found work and to this day has never received the recognition he deserved, because of his name.

One lesson to take from this story is the determining factor that character, rather than background or upbringing, can have over a person's life. Two more starkly different lives can hardly be found than those shown in the behaviour, and in the fates, of the Göring brothers.

CHAPTER 37

JEAN BART

Dunkirk is well known to the British for very good reason. Less well known to the Brits, but not to the Dunkerquois, is the story of Jean Bart, the foremost French corsair. When this part of coastal northern France belonged to the Spanish Netherlands, Jean Bart was born into a sea-faring family. Aged twelve, he joined the Dutch Navy to fight the British, who were occupying Dunkirk.

He learned his trade with the Dutch and learned it well. But soon enough Dunkirk was French and in 1672 the war between France and the United Provinces of the Netherlands began, so he fought for the French. Denied a commission, as this was then restricted to the nobility, he became a privateer.

In the Nine Years' War, most easily understood as France against all comers, he distinguished himself. First, captured by the English, he was imprisoned at Plymouth. He and a small band of comrades not only escaped – they returned to France, rowing to Brittany in a stolen rowing boat.

Second, he showed the reach of the French Navy in a manner that the cynical might think deliberately designed to put the wind up his opponents. Breaking the Dunkirk blockade, he sailed to Scotland, burning villages before popping home again. If he could get there, people on the coasts of the British Isles must have thought, he could get anywhere.

Third, he was similarly a terror to the Dutch. With a small fleet of six vessels, he again smashed through a blockade, captured 130 ships loaded with wheat and returned them to famine-struck France, where the starving people of Paris cried out in the streets at the news of his success. Louis XIV realised Bart's merits, made him a commodore and raised him to the nobility. He went on to become an admiral.

The Peace of Ryswick put paid to Bart's active service – visions of a buccaneering admiral morosely scuffing the turf with his hands in his pockets, muttering, *Bedknobs and Broomsticks*-style, 'We ain't gonna have no fun no more' are plainly impertinent.

Sadly, he died young in 1702, aged fifty-one. He is, of course, buried in Dunkirk.

Over the years, fully thirty ships of the French Navy have been proud to bear the name Jean Bart. As I say, it is strange that he is so little known by us Brits. Heaven forbid it's because he always came out on top! You can think of all this the next time you are in Dunkirk's Place Jean-Bart, listening to the belfry play the Jean Bart tune, eating the chocolate, coffee cream and almond biscuits known as '*doigts de Jean Bart*'.

CHAPTER 38

THE FALCON OF MALTA

The siege of Malta had many heroes. The island was awarded a collective George Cross by George VI for its courageous resistance against Germany. Here, we look at the story of one of those heroes: George Beurling, the Falcon of Malta.

Though he had plenty of flying hours when war was declared and he had passed commercial pilot exams, Beurling's native Canadian Air Force required academic qualifications he lacked, so the determined Beurling took the hazardous sea journey to the UK* to join the RAF. His trainer paid tribute to Beurling's skills as a pilot, and the fact that he was a great shot. Importantly for our purposes, he was also brave as hell.

Soon he was flying Supermarine Spitfires, escorting bombers and flying fighter missions. He claimed his first kill over the Channel. But he was not to remain on British duties for long. Volunteering without knowing where he was going, he was soon posted to Malta. Three days after he arrived on the island, Beurling and his comrades were in action against German Messerschmitts, and he chalked up his first Maltese score: a 'damaged' rather than a 'kill'.

---

* Twice; he forgot his birth certificate the first time.

(Witnesses were required for accreditation of these things and he didn't have them for this one.)

Thereafter, the Beurling spree got going in earnest. Mostly in combat against Italian fighters, he notched up five kills in four days. A further two came a couple of days later. Beurling's fame began to spread. Inevitably, it wasn't all one way: as he was significantly shot up on several occasions, we can add luck to his attributes, as he emerged unscathed each time. He got partial credit on an Italian bomber and was awarded the Distinguished Flying Medal (DFM). Then came his biggest day: on 27 July 1942, he shot down two Italian Macchis and two Messerschmitts. One of each was flown by the man reckoned to be amongst the best of the Italian and German pilots respectively. A bar was added to his DFM.

A bout of dysentery had him bedbound for some time, and soon after he returned to active duty he was shot down, crash-landing on the island with nothing but a small cut on his arm to show for it. He merrily hitchhiked back to base. Several more kills later, he received the Distinguished Flying Cross. This crash-landing incident was one of the four occasions on which he was shot down over Malta. The fourth and last time was in the course of the Maltese defence; he baled out over the sea and had injuries to his torso, his foot and his arm. Sent back to the UK to convalesce, the aeroplane he was aboard crash-landed; Beurling was one of the few survivors.

Why was he so good? Fast reflexes, certainly. Strong nerves, definitely – especially as he made a habit of engaging at very close quarters, which most other pilots would avoid, contributing to his high kill count. But he also had great dedication. He thought non-stop about his craft, seeking and yearning to improve at every turn. He didn't engage in the off-duty high jinks with which so many pilots, then and after, have famously relieved the huge stress of fighter combat. Whatever factors we might credit for his success, his twenty-seven kills made him the most successful defender of Malta in a conflict that was decided in the air. He received the Distinguished Service Order on 4 November 1942.

War is a horrible business. We remember that each of these boasted 'kills' had other people on the receiving end. No man is an island and so on. But we also remember that but for men like Beurling, Malta would have fallen to the control of evil fascists.

After Malta, Beurling's fame was deployed by his superiors; he was tasked with promoting the sale of War Bonds. This didn't last long.

Though in some ways a poster boy for the armed forces, a teetotaller entirely focused on his work, he was given to excessively blunt remarks, telling his audiences how much he enjoyed killing people. So, he returned to squadron duties – but training others, not fighting, now.

Away from the frontline, Beurling's thirst for adrenaline-pumping moments had less productive outcomes. Stunts and tricks in the air became his passion, and he was much criticised. He was moved around a great deal. Reading between the lines, it's clear that those commanding him didn't quite know what to do with this hero. Others would have been 'canned' for the insubordination he showed; Beurling, they just kept moving.

A short stint back on frontline duties saw his final kill before his discharge in 1944. He unsuccessfully tried to join the United States Air Force. Forever keen to return to the thick of things, he joined the Israeli Air Force when the war ended – but he was not destined to fight for them. After a test flight, Beurling crashed his plane in Rome when coming in to land – less than a week after Israel had declared its independence. His luck had finally run out: his tenth crash was his last.*

He is buried in Israel, a proud and independent-minded country that chose well when taking on this stubborn warrior spurned by the others he had served. His story did not get the final glory he would have wanted. But he will always be remembered as the Falcon of Malta.

---

* The cause or causes of the crash are unclear. Allegations of sabotage have been persistent but remain unsubstantiated.

CHAPTER 39

AFRICA'S FIRST BISHOP

Ajayi was a slave. But thanks to some British officers, not for long.

Being a grandson of the King of the Oyo people did not help Ajayi nor his family when Fulani slave traders came to their village in early 1821.* Along with the rest of their village, he and his mother were taken into slavery. He never saw his father again – he was likely killed by the Fulani in the raid. Britain had outlawed slavery before Ajayi was born, but Spain and Portugal continued to use slaves in their American colonies. Ajayi and his fellow captives were sold to traders by the Fulani and were aboard a Portuguese ship soon to sail when the Royal Navy intervened. HMS *Myrmidon*,† under the command of Henry Leeke (later an MP for Dover), was part of the West Africa Squadron enforcing the British ban on slavery. The *Myrmidon* captured the slave ship, freed the slaves and put them ashore in Sierra Leone.

Freetown was a thriving colony, with the beautiful St George's Cathedral (which I visited when in Sierra Leone with the Conservative Party's Project Umubano) being

---

* This took place in what is modern-day Nigeria.
† The second Royal Navy ship to bear this name, the *Myrmidon* was a *Hermes*-class sloop-of-war. The *Hermes* herself was burnt in Alabama in 1814, to prevent her from falling into American hands.

built at around the time Ajayi and the others arrived there. In Freetown, Ajayi was under the care of the Church Missionary Society (CMS). He learned English and converted to Christianity. He took the name Samuel Crowther, after one of the CMS's founders. He got married (to a woman also freed from slavery) and applied himself to the study of theology.

Ordained by the Bishop of London, he opened a Christian mission in modern-day Nigeria. There, he translated the Bible into Yoruba and produced primers for both the Igbo and Nupe languages. Twenty years after his ordination, he became the first African bishop of the Anglican church. He became a Doctor of Divinity, the Oxford University part of his education being a rare bad mark for him. Queen Victoria recalled his recitation of the Lord's Prayer as being 'mellifluous'.

We can imagine the very different life this gentle man of God would have had but for his freedom being restored by the Royal Navy when he was a boy. Ajayi Samuel Crowther had a rich legacy – linguistic, theological and lineal. His grandson, Herbert, was one of the founders of Nigeria's independence movement. Next, we will look at the story of his great-great-great-granddaughter, who lived up to his legacy in the most wonderful way.

CHAPTER 40

A DOCTOR ACTS

Our heroine, Ameyo Adadevoh, is the great-great-great-granddaughter of Ajayi Samuel Crowther from our last story. She was a brilliant doctor. Having studied in London, for twenty years she was a leading practitioner in Nigeria. Always at the sharp end of the treatment of infectious diseases, Dr Adadevoh was the first to raise the alarm when swine flu hit her country in 2012. But her finest hour was yet to come.

During a 2014 strike by Nigerian doctors, Dr Adadevoh kept treating patients – thank goodness. Because in her clinic a Liberian, Patrick Sawyer, arrived convinced that he had malaria.

He didn't.

Sawyer was in fact Nigeria's Ebola patient zero. He was keen to get treated and get away to his important work. His government wanted that, too. Dr Adadevoh was pushed to release him back to his work – including receiving representations from the Liberian ambassador to do so. This was in an environment, remember, that hadn't yet seen Ebola, so – just as in the preliminary stages of other viruses we might consider – many would have thought any other course alarmist.

Instead, as many of her colleagues continued on strike,

Dr Adadevoh insisted on isolating her patient. Lacking any of the relevant equipment, she put up wooden screens – we might even say a barricade – around the isolation area.* As she had done with swine flu before it, Dr Adadevoh was the first to raise the alarm over Ebola with her government, and she was the first to make the push for the relevant protective equipment whilst continuing to give first-class care to those in her charge.

By keeping Sawyer in quarantine against his and his government's wishes, Dr Adadevoh curbed a wider spread of the Ebola virus in Nigeria.

But not without cost.

In the course of caring for her patients, Dr Adadevoh herself contracted Ebola and died in August 2014 whilst in quarantine. The greatest tribute to her endeavours is one I think she would have chosen: her country was declared Ebola-free in the autumn of 2014. But for Dr Adadevoh, the spread of that most awful of diseases – and the lives of many thousands of her fellow Nigerians – would undoubtedly have been very different. I think Samuel Crowther would have been very proud of her.

---

* This story is told in the 2016 film *93 Days*.

CHAPTER 41

BISHOP BENNO DOESN'T LIKE
AN ARGUMENT

Bishop Benno of Osnabrück is sometimes called a saint. In that capacity, he is invoked against grasshoppers, against which he apparently had a strong hostile record. Niche, but useful in farming, I imagine. But today we interest ourselves in his ability to avoid an argument.

Benno was raised to the bishopric because he had been a military architect to Henry IV, the Holy Roman Emperor (those were the days, as far as interesting ecclesiastical promotional paths were concerned). He was loyal to his master, but Henry was having a bit of a problem with the Pope. In fact, Henry remained excommunicated for twenty-six years, so quite a lot of a problem in a society that looked to the papacy for leadership and guidance. Sure, plenty of Emperors were at odds with the Popes of their day, but Henry's decades-long stoush is unique amongst the medieval monarchs.

Benno knew which side his bread was buttered but hardly wanted to get caught between the two powerhouses. Things came to a head at Ticinum, now Pavia, where bishops opposed to Pope Gregory VIII gathered to use the nuclear option: remove the Pope; put a new one in.

Sure, Benno would go along with it in the end, but he certainly didn't want to front the campaign and would rather avoid talking about it at all, if you don't mind.

So it was that, in the church at Ticinum where things were being thrashed out by the multitude of bishops, he found himself earnestly praying for guidance by the altar, where he'd noticed there was a hole at the back. He got a bit closer. A bit closer still. Then, when nobody was looking, he popped himself inside the altar, pulled the altar cloth over the hole to hide it, and absented himself from proceedings altogether. And stayed there all day as the argument raged.

Surely we have all longed for a handy altar to hide in from time to time. Indeed, I imagine that in recent times, had they only known of his example, a number of congressmen and senators in Washington DC might have prayed to Benno. A more pious hideout it is difficult to imagine. Benno gave thanks to his maker for this miniature sanctuary, which happened to permit him to hear who was saying what in the debate amongst his brethren without participating in it himself.

In time, his absence from proceedings became known and all and sundry searched the town for him. Contemporary accounts claim that his blameless lodging house in town almost fell down with the weight of searchers trampling through it. He kept his head down and said his prayers.

Once the decision to renounce Pope Gregory and get a new Pope had finally been taken, Bishop Benno emerged from his place of rest when nobody was looking and resumed his prayers by the altar. Asked by the astonished crowd who finally realised his presence where he had been, he swore by all the saints that he had never left the church. Which, of course, was true.

Bishop Benno took his lesson to heart, as when he got back to Osnabrück he had a new altar just like Ticinum's fashioned for his church. Thus did Benno remain on good terms with not one but two Popes and an Emperor. Who is to say that his method was not wise in pursuit of his aim, 'To live peaceably with all men'?

Grasshopper banishment is all well and good, but I say that he would make an excellent patron saint of those sought out by lobbyists.

CHAPTER 42

CLIVE'S GREATEST VICTORY

Clive of India was a servant of Empire and of profit – the sort whose statues are targeted by vandals today. Pitt the Elder called him a 'heaven-born general'; plainly enough to get him double-cancelled in the modern era. But his greatest success should be uncontroversial even to the Year Zero crowd.

In the mid-1700s, Clive was working for the East India Company at Fort St George in Madras. There, he made friends with a chap called Maskelyne.

News from home was sporadic and people had the habit of reading letters they received to their friends. (For millennial readers: a 'letter' was a way people communicated in the olden days, using ink applied to paper. 'Letters' could be short like a text; long like an email; or even longer, like something to which you'd say 'TL;DR'.)

One day, Maskelyne read Clive a letter that the latter found so charming and perceptive that Clive returned to his friend a couple of days later to ask to hear it again. The letter was from Maskelyne's sister. Her miniature (a very small portrait) was on show in Maskelyne's room. Clive asked his friend if the portrait was accurate; he was told that it captured her appearance but couldn't possibly convey the excellence of her character. You know me well, said Clive. Write to your sister and tell her about me. For I would like her to come to India to marry me.

So, Maskelyne put pen to paper and made his friend's case so persuasively that Miss Maskelyne was convinced to travel to the other side of the world to meet someone she might marry. And she did.

Beats Tinder, doesn't it?

CHAPTER 43

WASHINGTON'S HORSES

Before he was America's first President, George Washington was of course one of his nascent country's most successful military leaders.*

Washington had two favourite horses. (Thomas Jefferson claimed that Washington was the best horseman of his age. Acceptable flattery; no doubt, he was good.) The first, Blueskin, is the horse you see in all the portraits. Blueskin was a fine parade horse, large and elegant. The second, Nelson, was a smaller, sturdy steed, calm under fire. Washington always mounted this horse when action was likely.

His men took to noting each morning which horse their general was to ride, and from this, word swiftly made its way through the ranks as to what sort of day it would be.

There is an obvious lesson here – that the approach or tool needed for action may be less flashy than the one that catches the eye. But I want to make a different point, too.

---

* In the Newburgh Letter of 1782, the army proposed to Washington that he should become King of America. He declined this suggestion as he declined to serve more than two terms as President. In both cases, this leader made great and self-effacing decisions that set the course for his new country.

Leaders, not just *including* but *especially* those trusted implicitly by those who follow them, must be acutely aware of the fact that even the smallest of their deeds will be monitored for signs of what is to come.

CHAPTER 44

BUDGE BUDGE

This is the story of Strachan's magnificent binge.

During Clive of India's Calcutta campaign of 1756–57, one obstacle on the way to Calcutta was a fort at Baj-Baj, which the Brits wittily called Budge Budge – fittingly, as it had proven hitherto unbudgeable, resisting both bombardment by ships and attacks on land.

So, a large naval force was tasked with dealing with Budge Budge. They moored up at a safe distance nearby and their commanders set about finalising the plan of attack for the following day. Some 250 sailors were to join a storming party, supported by heavy guns.

But this plan reckoned without Able Seaman Strachan.

Unusually for a sailor, Able Seaman Strachan was apparently fond of a drink. The night before the battle, he was doing some serious preloading. When sufficiently fired up, he weaved his way up to the fort, climbed the wall and started setting to around him when the defenders belatedly clocked the presence of this quixotic lone warrior. Strachan pre-emptively gave himself three cheers and cried out, 'The place is mine!' – but in fact the tide was turning against him (not least as he snapped his sword's blade off at the hilt, against foe or earthwork who can say).

Fortunately for him, drawn by the noise he was making, a couple of his mates turned up and swiftly shouted the odds with him.

Seeing that their hitherto impregnable fortress had apparently been breached, the entire garrison promptly fled. The storming force that scrambled as they belatedly realised that battle had been joined precipitately was largely unrequired. Thus, instead of the pitched battle that had been expected, the fort had fallen with a single British casualty. A captain, one Campbell by name, had been shot by his own side as they apparently thought him one of the enemy. How popular he had been with his men prior to this accident remains unknown.

Strachan was summoned before the admiral in charge of the Budge Budge expedition, Charles Watson.* What's all this then, Able Seaman? Well, I took the fort, didn't I? Aye, but on a frolic of your own, Strachan, a frolic of your own. Watson rebuked him for his rash actions, which could have had a very different outcome, for him and for others. Indeed, Strachan was seemingly left with the impression that when things had calmed down there would be a time in which his impulsiveness would be addressed in a distinctly disciplinary manner.

---

* Watson was a remarkable man in his own right. Detached from his fleet to patrol off Cadiz when treasure galleons from the Spanish Main were there for the taking – perhaps the most remunerative opportunity a sailor will have in his life – he nevertheless sailed to Toulon on news that a battle might take place, thinking his ship might be needed by the fleet. The extent to which this noted commander kept a stern face whilst laughing behind his hands in his interview with Strachan is an open question.

We know this as the last words known to history from the sadly under-documented Strachan are from his widely reported incredulous remarks made to his mates after the meeting: 'Why, if I'm flogged for this, I'll never take another fort alone as long as I live!'

CHAPTER 45

WHERE THE HEART FLIES

Robert the Bruce* died of leprosy (or not, depending on who you believe, but anyway, he died). His heart was removed and put in a silver casket, which his faithful supporter James Douglas sought to take to Jerusalem, where Robert had wished to make pilgrimage.

Alas, Douglas got into a scrap in Spain and was, depending on your preference, caught in a weak spot in battle or deserted on the field by his Spanish allies. Hard-pressed by enemies all around him, Douglas took the casket from the chain around his neck, threw it into the horde pressing upon him – towards Jerusalem, I like to think – and cried, and I paraphrase slightly, 'Lead us as you always did – I follow you, or I die!'

Sadly for Douglas, it was Option B.

Both Douglas's body and the heart were recovered from the battlefield by their allies in due course. Douglas was buried at Dunfermline Abbey, where Bruce's body lay, and in accordance with his wishes, Bruce's heart was interred at Melrose Abbey, where it was rediscovered in the 1990s and reburied with a new marker in 1998.

---

* Who, whilst regarded in the modern age as a hero amongst Scots, has a record that is far from clear: together with his friend Kirkpatrick, he murdered powerful noble John Comyn in a church in Dumfries in order to become King.

CHAPTER 46

THE FIRST FEMALE DOCTOR?

The suffragist Elizabeth Garrett Anderson is famous for being the first woman to qualify in Britain as a physician and surgeon. It is with some trepidation that I suggest that this widely held belief about the excellent Garrett Anderson is untrue.

Born in Ireland, graduating from the University of Edinburgh's medical school in 1812 and passing the Royal College of Surgeons' examination in 1813, Dr James Barry was inspector general of the British Army – the second highest position in our military to which a doctor can rise, equivalent in rank to a brigadier general.

After joining the army, Barry's first posting was to Cape Town. He formed a close relationship with the governor of the Cape, Lord Charles Somerset, after successfully treating his sick daughter. In a ten-year stint in the Cape, Barry performed what was probably the first Caesarean section in Africa in which mother and child both survived. The child was named after Barry, as were several subsequent children delivered by Caesareans – one of whom, James Barry Hertzog, became Prime Minister of South Africa.

Leading an eventful life both in medicine and otherwise,

Barry argued with Florence Nightingale,* fought a duel with pistols with a captain of the Light Dragoons, caught yellow fever in the West Indies and dealt with a cholera outbreak in Malta. Soldiers wherever Barry was posted throughout the Empire loved the doctor who pushed for improvements in their diet and treatment.

All well and good, but 'So what?' I hear you ask. Well, Barry was born a woman.

This was not revealed until after death, when Barry's body was laid out. The British Army – which at that time did not require a medical examination for those joining up as officers – sealed all Barry's records, and they remained sequestered for over 100 years.

James Barry was born Margaret Ann Bulkley and successfully lived as a man from 1809 until death in 1865, gaining access to medical school, graduating, serving in the forces, helping thousands through medicine and hygiene and living a life of adventure to the full. The estimable Garrett Anderson received her licence in 1865, fully fifty years after Barry qualified.

The lesson from this story, as we consider the examples of Barry and Garrett Anderson together? Sometimes, unjustifiable prejudices can stop you living your life as you would wish. Protest and subversion are different, but both reasonable, responses to it. Up to you.

---

* Were it not for the revered status she justly enjoys, we might resort to the vernacular and say that Barry is 'thoroughly slagged off' in Nightingale's memoirs.

CHAPTER 47

STERN DAUGHTER OF THE VOICE OF GOD

I have this story from Mario Monti, former European Commissioner and technocratic Prime Minister of Italy.

Shortly after she was toppled from power in the UK, Margaret Thatcher gave a speech in Italy, taking questions afterwards. Her audience asked her why she was so Eurosceptic; she turned the tables, asking them why they liked the European Union so much.

Monti said, well, it provides a requirement for fiscal stability and prudence, restraint, sensible economic policy, limiting debt to manageable levels and so forth.

Thatcher rejoined: so you need the EU to *tell you* to do that which you know you should do already but lack the strength of will to do yourself?

Monti, disarmingly, said, 'Yes.'

Thatcher: well, then now you know why the British do not need the EU. Because they have *me*.

* * *

A second anecdote. I took a friend to an event in London at which Thatcher was the guest of honour. In person, she had that effect that really very few have on a public gathering – the moment she was in the room it felt like it had tipped over slightly, with all the attention going to one corner like a pinball table on tilt.

My friend was a big Thatcher fan. He met her, and, eminent lawyer though he was, he couldn't get his words out. Thatcher held his hand and waited – for a minute. This may not sound like long, but it is FOR EVER in real time.

In the end he blurted out: 'You saved our country!'

She carried on holding his hand, looking him in the eye, and replied slowly, in a low voice: 'I agree.'

* * *

A third.

Former Prime Minister of France Michel Rocard was fond of telling this story about the Iron Lady. As he urged the case for the UK to join the (as it was then) European single currency, Thatcher apparently told him, 'Not in a thousand years.'

Rocard replied, 'Fantastic! So it's not about the principle – it's just a question of timing!'

CHAPTER 48

BEWARE THE LARGE IRONIC OBJECT

John Roebling was a noted engineer who left his native Prussia, which valued militarism above all things, to seek swifter and greater advancement in his profession in the New World. He found it.

The crossing between the two proud cities of Brooklyn and New York* was made by ferry for many years. As the cities expanded, so did the traffic. The ferries were crowded, unhygienic and unsafe. A bridge was called for. It would require one of the magnificent new designs called 'suspension bridges'.

Work began in 1869. The Brooklyn Bridge would be the longest suspension bridge in the world when it was built, so it was quite a challenge. Moreover, the bridge would have to rest on caissons, within the narrow, hollow centres of which workers dug out sediment from the river bottom in unpleasant, confined conditions. This compressed environment underwater gave some men 'the bends', a condition not well understood at the time, which they called 'caisson disease'. Three men died and over a hundred were treated for the horrible condition.

They were not the bridge's only casualties. One day,

---

* Brooklyn was not consolidated into New York as one of its five boroughs until 1898.

gazing out over the scene that would host his crowning achievement, Roebling neglected to notice the ferry coming in – hardly a small object, after all – and the very ship his design would eliminate crushed his toes against the wharf. Ouch to the power of ten on the irony scale, but even at that time modern medicine could have come to his aid.

However, once his toes were amputated, Roebling insisted that his maker and the healing power of water would give him all the help he needed.

He got tetanus and died.*

So, the bridge was to be finished by John's son, Washington, a distinguished veteran of the Civil War who had been at the Battles of Antietam and Gettysburg. But he too fell victim to caisson disease and was never well again for the rest of his days. So, much of the work to complete the bridge was executed by his wife, Emily, whilst Washington observed the site by telescope. Emily campaigned for greater recognition for Washington, especially given the sacrifices he had made for the project, but in truth she was as responsible for its completion as anyone by the time that it was done. Fittingly, she was the first to cross the completed bridge.

Two lessons from this story, I think: first, having a grand vision is all well and good, but do look where you're going. Second, piety is to be admired, but should you harbour such a profound faith then consider that perhaps God gave you medicine, too.

---

* In his partial defence, 'water therapy' or hydrotherapy was heavily promoted in the 1800s.

Postscript. The bridge ruined this branch of the family, but they weren't the only Roeblings to suffer in the vanguard of their age's grand new feats of engineering. Washington had a namesake nephew. The younger Washington Roebling went down with the *Titanic*.

Second postscript. Niggling public concerns about the safety of the then novel bridge were not helped by a stampede of pedestrians in which a dozen people died. So, the ever enterprising P. T. Barnum secured a PR coup by walking the famous Jumbo and a score of his fellow elephants over the bridge to demonstrate its loadbearing strength. Circus promotion doubling up as public service… genius.

CHAPTER 49

OUR MOST DECORATED OFFICER NEVER FIRED A SHOT

Most of these episodes bring unknown stories to light. I suppose that this is not the case here, as our hero is one who never fired a shot but who has more war memorials than anyone else – but that fame was won for good reasons and ones worth rehearsing.

This is the story of Noel Chavasse, VC *and bar*. Which means he won two Victoria Crosses. In a conflict that saw much exceptional service and heroism, no other man won two VCs in the First World War (and only two others have received two, ever). Chavasse was a doctor at the Battle of the Somme, the Battle of Guillemont, where he was wounded, the Battle of Passchendaele and the Battle of Pilckem Ridge, where he died of wounds. In each conflict, he exposed himself to great danger to save others, ultimately at the cost of his life.

He was also an Olympian and took a first-class degree from (nobody's perfect) Oxford. He had only been a doctor for two years before he went to war. Like so many, his was a young life given selflessly for others and for his country. In a war that saw so much bravery and took so much from Britain, he was our most highly decorated officer.

Before his VCs, he had already won the Military Cross for gallantry and been mentioned in dispatches, both in 1915. Several times he went out into no-man's land, the most dangerous circumstances – more than once almost up to the enemy trench itself – to help wounded soldiers. After one failed push, he worked to save men through a long night, close to enemy lines and under sniper fire. This sort of bravery is hard for us to imagine, but we must remember that when called upon our armed forces still deliver it with the same ageless courage.

Chavasse was a twin; his older (by twenty minutes) brother, Christopher, was in no particular order the Bishop of Rochester, an Olympian like Noel, a winner of the Military Cross and the Croix de Guerre and the first master of St Peter's College, Oxford, which was founded by their father.

Noel was engaged to one of his cousins, Frances Chavasse (known by her middle name, Gladys), who was herself mentioned in Second World War dispatches at Monte Cassino, which was no gentle affair. His nephew, Christopher's son, was named in his honour; the younger Noel Chavasse won the Military Cross and served under Montgomery. What a family.

The excellent Lord Ashcroft paid £1.5 million for his medals, which are now on display in the wonderful Imperial War Museum, an institution with a name so purely and absolutely outrageous to the woke it will probably survive these mad times as an exception to the rule.

Chavasse features on at least sixteen war memorials across his country. Perhaps you've seen one? Perhaps the most important, though, is not in the UK. It is at his grave, at Brandhoek, near Ypres, where uniquely his headstone bears the image of two Victoria Crosses.

CHAPTER 50

SING US A SONG, YOU'RE A BELGIAN

Some of these stories are about great battles and events. Some are about whole lives. This one is about a single, disastrous moment.

It is apparent to those willing to dig beneath a seemingly placid exterior that Belgium is a country riven with simmering political strife. Made up of the southern bit of the old Netherlands, it is itself famously split on language and culture between the Flemish and the Walloons, with Brussels a peculiar pearl caught between them. They take this topic very seriously. Governments have (genuinely) fallen over language issues – what signs are used in villages, what languages are used in schools. I'm seeking to emphasise here that the language you speak is a big deal in that there Belgium. Oh, and thanks to this background, famously every conceivable group or gathering in the country has its own Parliament. Pity the Belgian estate agent who takes wide-eyed couples on property searches round the average Belgian semi, muttering 'kitchen, living room, debating chamber, Speaker's apartment...'

Anyway, Yves Camille Désiré Leterme is a silver fox and a former leader of the Christian Democratic and Flemish Party. He served twice as his country's Prime Minister (his first term falling between Guy Verhofstadt and Herman Van Rompuy...).

Here are some Leterme positives. He could manage a Budget, turning debt into a surplus. He has always been a strong and eloquent proponent of more autonomy for Flanders, which was his political mission. He always enjoyed a very strong level of personal support in elections. He was and is generally an assured media performer – an important quality in the present era. Admittedly, this was marred slightly by his suggestion in an interview that French speakers are apparently just not clever enough to speak Dutch. But generally, he could stick to his lines.

HOWEVER.

In 2007, he was having a tough interview on TV. The journalist, much to the disapproval of Emily Thornberry no doubt, started pub-quizzing him. He misstated the event celebrated on Belgium's national day,* which one might think he would know. He was, no doubt, rattled.

The journalist then asked, do you even know the Belgian national anthem in French? Why, *of course* I do. And he opened his mouth and began to sing... *La Marseillaise.*

---

* 21 July. It marks the coronation of the first monarch, King Leopold I – not, as Leterme answered, the proclamation of the constitution.

Now, don't get me wrong. *La Marseillaise* is a wonderful, rousing song. In *Casablanca*, it is the centrepiece of one of my favourite moments in one of my favourite films. But... it's the wrong song. And it's the anthem of... the wrong country.

My instinct on such occasions is to think of the poor staffer in the corner, head in hands. I prepped him, I prepped him... how could I have seen this coming? Well, you couldn't. We have all said the wrong thing from time to time. Found ourselves saying words we wish we could catch mid-air and stuff back into our mouths. But this was special. I've been trying to think of what the equivalent in Anglo politics might be. Not knowing the words of the national anthem for, say, a principality for which you have ministerial responsibility and therefore semi-mumbling, semi-mouthing instead of singing doesn't quite seem to match it. It's voluntarily singing the national anthem of *another country* when asked about your own. The closest I can get is Nicola Sturgeon giving a rousing rendition of 'Swing Low, Sweet Chariot' when asked what Scottish rugby fans like to sing at games. Even that doesn't seem to fit, albeit I'd like to see it.

Perhaps this moment inadvertently serves as a glorious demonstration of the diminishing importance of nation states in the EU. But for a politician whose whole career was based on saying that his own area should be treated as, or should actually *be*, a country, such a defence doesn't really work either.

Anyway, Leterme is still around, in business rather than politics, having retired young; the Belgian Tony Blair, I suppose. But gosh, I'd love him to do another interview and sing a bit. I just wouldn't want to be his staffer getting the call from the party chairman afterwards.

CHAPTER 51

THE MOST COMPLETE POSSIBLE VICTORY

Question: what is the most complete military victory possible? A question to which there is perhaps no right answer, but how's this: 'A battle you don't even have to fight yourself but win hands down.' This is the story of the Battle of Karánsebes.

Austria was at war with Turkey in 1788. The Austrian Army was on the march around Karánsebes (in present-day Romania). On one September evening, the Austrian Hussars crossed the Timiş river and, finding no enemies, promptly set up camp and had some drinks. In due course some infantrymen followed the Hussars over the river, sought to join in with the digestif consumption and were rebuffed. An argument began and, as Britney Spears would say, one thing led to another.

Disputes between booze-fuelled groups of men with guns are generally a bad idea. This was no exception. Soon, bullets were flying. Some wag cried out, 'Turks! Turks!' and soon enough everyone was legging it from the wholly absent Turkish Army. The Hussars sought to retreat to camp, where their unannounced gallop was interpreted as a cavalry attack and they were met with artillery fire.

The whole Austrian Army – some 100,000 men – was now in disarray. Things were not helped by the fact it was made up of an admirably heterodox grouping of different nationalities, each contingent of which had varying degrees of understanding with regard to the language of each of the others. Thus, men shouted words others did not understand and fired at every shadow – i.e. at their own comrades. A full-blown retreat from an imaginary enemy ensued. Emperor Joseph II was ignobly dismounted and thrown into a ditch in the confusion.

A couple of days later, the Ottomans arrived on the battlefield. One can only imagine their perplexity upon finding a shedload of dead Austrians. Good job, everyone, really well done, we pulled that off.

The Turks took Karánsebes with ease as a result. Losses were massively overstated in press reports shortly after the time, perhaps because neutral observers found the situation amusing and wanted a better punchline. Whatever the truth of it, casualties amongst the Austrian army certainly ran into the hundreds. Ottoman casualties – zero. Obviously.

How's that for a complete victory? Or perhaps we should say that the Austrians 'won' as well as lost?

CHAPTER 52

THE HEROINE OF WARSAW

This is the story of 'Little Wanda with the Braids', the Heroine of Warsaw.

Niuta Tajtelbaum, or Teitelbaum, fought in the Warsaw Uprising, personally destroying a heavy machine-gun nest and taking part in an attack on the German artillery pounding the Jewish ghetto. But she is best known for her part as an underground fighter in the communist People's Guard. She attacked German-only centres like cafés and cinemas, and her team sabotaged German supply lines.

In my favourite of these stories, she dressed herself in her favoured 'cover' attire, a Polish maiden's outfit, and strolled into a Gestapo building. She no doubt looked the picture of innocence. She smiled at the guards and politely asked for the name of a particular officer. Most likely thinking that this pretty woman was involved with said officer, the guards promptly ushered her in to see him. Meeting not one but three Nazis in the office she was shown to, she dispelled any notion of her harmlessness by producing a hidden pistol and shooting all three of them. Two died; one was wounded. So, she followed up, popping on a nurse's outfit and heading to the hospital, where she finished the job and killed the patient and his guard to boot. On another occasion, she led a People's

Guard attack on a German officers' club, killing four officers and wounding a further ten.

Perhaps inevitably given the risks she took, in the end the Gestapo caught this bravest of women. She had a poison pill but had no time to swallow it when they ambushed her. She was interrogated for weeks, tortured and killed. She never betrayed her comrades.

She was infamous amongst the German occupiers, who christened this phantom threat 'Little Wanda with the Braids'. Such figures are elevated to myth. They generate fear. Their opponents see them around every corner. Thus, the harm they do to their enemies resonates far beyond the deeds they actually do, penetrating their psyche. No less than the Nazis deserved.

But such figures do not deserve to be forgotten now themselves. This is just one story of many from the deeds of the ghetto girls – of the '*haluzzenmadein*' ('pioneer girls', a portmanteau from Hebrew and German). Judy Batalion's new book *The Light of Days*, the fruit of a dozen years of research by this granddaughter of Holocaust survivors, has many tales of these unjustly forgotten women, and I commend it to you.

CHAPTER 53

THE SINS OF THE FATHER

Spencer Perceval was, as every quizzer knows, the only British Prime Minister to be assassinated.

One day in May 1812, the PM was rushing to the Commons chamber when he was shot in the lobby by an aggrieved businessman, John Bellingham. Like the current MP for Northampton (North, in the current case), Perceval was a QC and a law officer in government, the only Solicitor General or Attorney General so far to become Prime Minister. Lawyers, it seems, are always in the boardroom but seldom get the big chair. He was Prime Minister for three years and prosecuted the Peninsular War that gave us the Die Hards and Rio as capital of Portugal (know your #deanehistory!). He had thirteen children, undertook much charitable work in his private life and was a leading proponent of the abolition of slavery. Perceval was nicknamed 'Little P' by contemporaries and in the press, rendering him to the 21st-century casual observer 10 Downing Street's least likely rapper.

After some considerable success as a defender of the government and prosecutor of its enemies, he became Chancellor of the Exchequer – a more conventional route to being Prime Minister. He gave up a lucrative legal practice to do so.

What of his killer?

Bellingham had been imprisoned by the Russians for five years over a deal gone wrong, and he blamed the British government for not bailing him out. When he got back, he repeatedly petitioned anyone he could think of about his case. Every door was closed to him.

Bellingham thought that he was being persecuted by the Russians as revenge for him exposing internal corruption. Plainly such a view is and always has been fanciful, and certainly there are no parallels here with anything that happens nowadays. Little did those rejecting this persistent petitioner appreciate the lengths to which he would go in his despair. He became a regular in the Public Gallery in the House of Commons, where once people could just wander in and watch debate without fuss, and popped along to a tailor who obligingly turned out a nice pocket for his suit for concealing firearms. In both respects, it was a different time.

He shot the PM through the heart and was hanged for it – within a week. After all, government was keen to quell any idea of a revolt, and in its defence, there were dozens of witnesses to the killing and only one suspect.

The conspiracy theories that surround the assassinations of other leaders were at least absent in this case... or so one might think. Rumours of an accomplice swirled for a while, without resolution. In any case, thus ended Spencer Perceval and John Bellingham. There is a memorial to Perceval in Westminster Abbey; a tribute not universally delivered to politicians.

Six years after the killing, and long before he became Prime Minister, one of Perceval's successors at No. 10, Lord Palmerston, narrowly avoided assassination too. The bullet grazed his back: his attacker was sent to an asylum and the sympathetic Palmerston paid for his legal bills. In more recent times, Irish Republican terrorists have sought to murder the Prime Minister and have successfully murdered more junior ministers. But, in the main, British Prime Ministers have not been subject to personal physical attacks in the same way that we see in some other countries.

Why do I mention this relatively well-known set of events in this volume, generally dedicated as it is to the obscure? Well, it's to do with the cancel culture we presently enjoy or endure, depending upon your perspective. The former MP and now peer Lord Bellingham is a direct descendant of John Bellingham. In this peculiar era in which people are punished for the sins of the fathers, presumably this means that despite his decades of public service, Lord Bellingham should be cancelled as an enthusiastic assassin.

Postscript. Small familial revenge was had at the 1997 election, when a descendant of Spencer Perceval stood for the Referendum Party against Henry Bellingham and won enough votes to cost Bellingham his North West Norfolk seat, which was therefore briefly held by the Labour Party. Bellingham regained it in 2001.

CHAPTER 54

THE LAST SAILING SHIP OF WAR

The *Pass of Balmaha* was British, to begin with. Built in Glasgow and launched in 1888, she was steel-hulled, a little over 1,500 tons and had three fine masts. Sold to Canadians just before the First World War, she was managed by Americans and understandably transferred to the (neutral) American registration and flag when hostilities commenced.

In June 1915, the *Pass of Balmaha* sailed for Arkhangelsk with a cargo of cotton. She was stopped by the British ship *Victorian* – which was an 'auxiliary cruiser', aka an armed merchantman – which is ironic given *Pass of Balmaha*'s destiny. A rather small prize crew of an officer and six marines were put aboard the *Pass of Balmaha*, with orders to sail to Orkney for inspection. The British ordered the American colours to be struck and replaced with the White Ensign. As this would mean his ship being a belligerent rather than flying neutral colours, *Pass of Balmaha*'s captain, one Scott by name, wasn't keen. But he did as he was told. Up it went, and up popped a German U-boat alongside her as if on cue in a bad joke.

Oh... sugar, Scott no doubt thought. Down with the British flag and up with the Stars and Stripes, and you Brits can hide yourselves below deck whilst we're inspected, with my grateful thanks for all your fantastic help.

The U-boat captain wasn't taken in by all this flag-switching and ordered *Pass of Balmaha* to sail to Germany for inspection. This Scott did, keeping the British shut up below decks on his way, as he had a fair idea what his vessel's fate would be thanks to them. Incidentally, *Pass of Balmaha* was the U-boat's last victim as she was sunk by British ship the *Prince Charles* later that day, so it wasn't all Germany's way. The *Prince Charles* was a so-called 'Q-ship' – a decoy designed to lure submarines into an attack on a seeming merchantman which was in fact heavily armed. The switching from civil to (disguised) military use is a theme here.

Pass of Balmaha got to Cuxhaven in north Germany without being waylaid yet again. The Americans were allowed to go on their way, but the ship was seized by the Germans. As for the erstwhile prize crew… the reaction of the small British contingent disembarking into the arms of their enemies remains unrecorded, but I imagine we might be able to guess it.

Any German ships that got past the British Navy's blockade struggled to resupply, given the scarcity of friendly or colonial ports to supply coal. So, despite the advances made in decades of naval warfare, a fighting sailing ship that didn't need any coal was thought at least worth a go. Thus, the *Pass of Balmaha* became SMS *Seeadler** and was

---

* Seeadler is the name of a white-tailed eagle in German.

equipped with a new, hidden auxiliary engine, two hidden 105mm guns, two hidden heavy machine guns and a pair of torpedo tubes. Suddenly this seemingly harmless sailing ship – disguised as a Norwegian merchantman – had more teeth than a crocodile!

Seeadler passed her first test – despite being boarded for inspection, she was allowed past the British blockade. Thereafter, like the *Emden* in Chapter 34, she led the Allies a merry dance whilst inflicting great harm on our merchant shipping.

Fifteen ships fell to the *Seeadler* over the course of the next seven months or so. British, French, Italian and (once they were in the war) American ships – each time incredulous that this ship of sail was in fact ready to blow them out of the water if they didn't surrender, which they always did. So convincing was the *Seeadler*'s disguise that the last-minute unfurling of the hostile flag and the demand to stop was sometimes disbelieved. The captain of one of her victims even had himself rowed over to her, so convinced was he that it was a fellow merchantman pranking him.

In all her captures, most of which were sunk after their crews were taken off, the *Seeadler* caused one single fatality, and that was by accident – firing a single shot at a British ship to stop her and take out her radio capability (which worked), a steam pipe ruptured and killed a British sailor. That's it. All the other crews were taken off their vessels safely. Indeed, *Seeadler*'s biggest problem was what to do with all her prisoners. Periodically, this gentleman raider of the sea would stop a ship and disgorge all her prisoners onto the prize rather than sinking her, ordering the captured vessel to put to port… not, of course, without first ensuring that sufficient equipment had been removed, so as to enable the *Seeadler* to get away before her released captive could report her to the Allies.

And this all worked, for when the end for the *Seeadler* came it was not at the hands of the Allies but at Mopelia* in the Society Islands, where a wave threw her against a reef and she was destroyed. Miraculously, all hands and prisoners survived.

The absence of a ship would end most such stories. But the gallant crew of the *Seeadler* was not done yet. The captain, Felix von Luckner, split his crew. He sailed with five men in an open boat via the Cook Islands towards Fiji, where he intended to capture a sailing ship, return to Mopelia for the rest of his crew and resume raiding.

They reached Atiu Island and pretended to be Dutchmen crossing the Pacific for a bet. I don't know about you, but I would have been sceptical. Luckily for them, as we all know New Zealanders are sports mad and the administrator ('resident') of the island was a Kiwi. So, they were given enough supplies to reach the next island in the group, Aitutaki. There, these masters of disguise pretended to be Norwegians. The resident Kiwi this time was more sceptical, but they were armed men of war and he wasn't. He couldn't hold on to them. So Luckner quickly made off to Rarotonga, where he

---

* Also known as 'Maupihaa', this is a beautiful and pretty much deserted atoll-style island.

thought he'd sighted an enemy (well, perhaps, but whilst he couldn't see this in the dark, in fact the ship was beached). So, he pushed on to Wakaya Island. This is over 2,000 miles in an open boat from where he began.

They tried the Norwegian gambit again, but this time someone saw through them, and the police came from Levuka. They threatened to blow Luckner out of the water. Not realising that the police were in fact unarmed, and not wishing to risk loss of life amongst the people now pressing around their ship, at last the plucky half-dozen German voyagers surrendered. Their odyssey was over. Von Luckner, later a successful public speaker, spent the rest of war as a POW in New Zealand (escaping once only to be recaptured).

But we're not done. Do you remember the rest of the crew we left back on Mopelia? A French trading ship, the *Lutece*, anchored off the reef. Informed of their gallant captain's capture by radio, the *Seeadler*'s remnant crew sailed out to *Lutece* and captured her. The crew of the *Lutece* was put ashore with the *Seeadler*'s prisoners from earlier prizes and sinkings, and the Germans set course for South America in the *Lutece*, which, thanking their luck, they renamed the *Fortuna*.

Alas, at least some of the luck was bad. The *Fortuna* struck uncharted rocks off Easter Island, where the crew survived wrecking yet again but were captured by the neutral Chileans once ashore and were interned for the remainder of the war. Finally, the escapades of both the *Seeadler* and her crew were over.

But their story wasn't. The crew's departure in the *Lutece / Fortuna* had left one last open boat at Mopelia. The captain of one of *Seeadler*'s victims took it with three other sailors and travelled 1,000 miles to Pago Pago. Thus, the Allies were finally brought up to date on the *Seeadler*, and the rescue of the remaining captured and stranded sailors on Mopelia was arranged.

One ship, but 100 stories, it seems. No doubt the strands of stories go on from each of these sailings, captures, sinkings and so on down to our present day. But thus ended the tale of one of the last sailing fighting ships of the First World War.

CHAPTER 55

CAESAR MEANS IT

We have discussed the plague that is piracy in previous stories. In this story we go back a little earlier, to the time just before the coming of Christ.

Southern Anatolia, now Turkey, was home to some tough hombres: Cilician pirates. In 75 BC, they captured a young Roman nobleman in the Aegean Sea – unfortunately for them, it was one Julius Caesar.

When Caesar was told that the Cilicians were ransoming him for twenty talents (i.e. a lot), he upbraided them and demanded that they seek a higher ransom. Why, you should demand at least fifty talents for me! This, it was obvious, was not a normal hostage. With the pirates' agreement, his servants were released to gather the ransom from his family and friends.

Caesar was, as soon became apparent to the pirates, quite the eccentric. He showed no fear of his captives, reciting the lengthy odes he was composing to / at them and rehearsing his political speeches before them, castigating them as a bad and ignorant audience if they didn't applaud sufficiently. He vigorously joined in with their games. He treated them like people who fell somewhere between his friends and his servants. But don't you worry, he told his captors and new playmates as they cavorted during the wait for the big payout: we're having fun now, but once I'm released, I'll come back and crucify the lot of you! Oh, how they laughed.

A month or so later, the ransom arrived and Caesar was released. At this young age, Caesar held no public office – but still, somehow, he promptly raised a strong Roman force and returned to the island and captured his erstwhile captors. He turned the pirates over to the authorities, but the Roman governor responsible seemed uncertain about how to punish them. After all, they hadn't been that bad to Caesar, and it could trigger problems with others in Anatolia; anything for a quiet life and so forth.

So, in an early example of cutting through red tape and rendering a bureaucratic process redundant, Caesar headed down to the prison with his men and promptly crucified them all.

A lesson widely applicable to dealing with people from commerce to despotism – when it comes to threats, don't seek to parse what someone says. Take it at face value. No matter how much they seem friendly, seem the sort of fellow with whom you can do business, no matter how *outré* or outlandish you think the threat to be... act as if they mean it. Because they probably do.

CHAPTER 56

WILLIAM THE EXPLODER

Long have we been fascinated by those who spontaneous-ly combust – or, as the subtitle of my sadly never written book on the subject has it: 'People who go pop'. Admit-tedly, the point with spontaneous combustion is that the poor victim is alive when it happens, rather than the bang coming post-mortem. But the explosion of the dead is still pretty striking.

It is therefore strange that one of the most famous people in history is not better known for having had this unusual explosive quality. William the Conqueror, or William the Bastard, depending on your perspective, was the Norman who famously conquered England and the Saxons. He died after being thrown against the pommel of his saddle whilst riding his horse – but not straight away.

The damage done to William's internal organs was sig-nificant, and he was a while a-dying; he used the time left to him to split his lands between his children – Norman-dy for his first born, Robert, but England to his second surviving son, William Rufus. No sooner can you say 'primogeniture' than this legacy was causing problems amongst those he left behind, and this long-running fa-milial dispute – which led to war between the siblings and their followers – is what has seized so much attention about William's demise. Fairly so – the fate of nations was swayed by that decision. But there is a more immediate and gruesome point to be recalled, too.

By some oversight, the sarcophagus made to receive William's remains was relatively narrow and William – how to put it? – well, after a lifetime of good royal living, William was *not* narrow. And after death, the gases within him swelled him yet more. Efforts to force him into the sarcophagus in the abbey church at Caen probably lacked the dignity expected for a King. The result certainly did.

BOOM went William.

Chroniclers of the day try, but struggle, to convey the stench of days-old putrid gut gases suddenly exposed to air and their effect upon the congregation pressed close around the scene – which, let us not forget, whilst no doubt a scene of mourning was also one of the great society affairs of the day. The presiding clergyman, it is said, set a new record for the speed with which he completed the remaining ceremonial rites. As you would, if assailed with the rotten remains of a King popped directly beneath your nose. So much for the glory of divine right. (Side note: in this vein the philosopher Diogenes was much given to teasing Alexander the Great,* once telling him that he had searched for his celebrated father's remains but could not distinguish Philip II's bones from those of a slave.)

---

* A privilege reserved for the very brave or the very foolish. To his credit, Alexander saw the genius in this idling philosopher and tolerated him to an extent few would ever have expected. Indeed, one day Alexander said to him, 'If I were not Alexander then I would wish to be Diogenes.' Diogenes replied, 'If I were not Diogenes then I, too, would wish to be Diogenes.'

Lesson? We are all mortal and all leave this world as we arrived in it, no more and no less than any other. William's body showed this base fact perhaps a little sooner, and more dramatically, than even Diogenes, bluntest of men, ever thought to point out.

CHAPTER 57

HE PASSED THIS WAY

Vilnius is of course the capital of present-day Lithuania and was one of the powerhouses in the Polish–Lithuanian Commonwealth that once dominated its region – a million-square-mile* giant now largely forgotten. Moreover, it's the birthplace of Captain Marko Ramius of *The Hunt for Red October*.

But in between the glory days of the Commonwealth and its modern-day renaissance, this Baltic city was a place on the way to other places that were at war with one another. There is a monument there today which tells that story.

On the western side of the monument, which one would pass on the way to Moscow, is a plaque: 'Napoleon Bonaparte passed this way in 1812 with 400,000 men.'

On the other side, a second plaque: 'Napoleon Bonaparte passed this way in 1812 with 9,000 men.'

Lesson: when people say not to underestimate the Russian winter, you should listen.

---

* Like so many countries, borders fluctuated – but this is an accurate reflection of its size at its height in the early 1600s.

CHAPTER 58

YOGI AND THE BOMB

Tensions were running high in 1962 during the Cuban Missile Crisis – right around the world but especially amongst those tasked with defending the United States.

Based on intelligence and projections of enemy activities, authorities in the USA not only believed that the USSR was willing to strike first but also that sleeper agents in the United States itself would likely be activated prior to such an attack in order to sabotage America's nuclear capabilities.

Thus it was that, in the small hours of the morning of 25 October 1962, the security facilities at the Duluth Sector Direction Center in Minnesota were on high alert. After all, the centre provided command and control over both aircraft squadrons and radar facilities in the region. We can imagine how a guard on duty in those circumstances felt in the moment at which he saw a shadowy figure climbing the far-off security fence in the darkness. Why, he was defending his base, his country, western civilisation from the Soviet threat... and here was an intruder.

So, he shot at the figure in the darkness and sounded the base's alarm, which warned of an attempted forcible entry. In turn, this set off the alarms in a relay at other relevant nuclear-related bases.

Volk Field is not close to Duluth. Indeed, it's in another state, Wisconsin, some 300 miles away. And significantly, it lacked a control tower – so its nuclear-armed F-106A jets were launched based on orders from Duluth. Unfortunately, the alarm system at Volk Field was not working properly that night, so Duluth's alert, rather than warning of potential on-site sabotage, sounded the base's klaxon instead. Oh, no biggie, that just orders nuclear-armed interceptor jets to take off.

Because of the global situation, America's defences were at DEFCON 3. So everyone knew that there were to be no drills. This, the pilots and their ground crews must have thought, is it. Nuclear war. They took to the runways.

However. Sometimes, no matter how finely honed a system may be, no matter how many times you've rehearsed for this moment... well, it doesn't hurt to check. Volk Field's commander telephoned his counterpart at Duluth. Not only, it emerged, was it supposed to be the sabotage alarm and not the take-off-and-kill-everything klaxon that was triggered but the 'intruder' was, in fact, a bear. (I didn't know how prominent a role bears were going to play in these stories when I began writing them.)*

That's all well and good, super news and so forth, but... the planes were already on the runway with orders to go to war. In a demonstration of the rule that no matter how

---

* At the time of the Cold War, one would have to be careful even saying, 'It was a bear' over the telephone. Replacing the Tu-4 (which was a reverse-engineered version of the American B-29 copied from crashed aircraft), the capacious and tough Tupolev 95 was the leading Soviet bomber from the mid-1950s onwards, so it was in service at this point – as it is to this day – and is called 'The Bear'.

many flash-bang systems you've got, in the end, sometimes you've just got to do the thing yourself, the base command centre emptied of officers, who got into cars and promptly drove onto the runway.

Admittedly, the F-106As were interceptors, not bombers. But their launch would have been noticed by the USSR, and in the heightened tensions of the day that might have led to anything.

Thus we can say that some initiative, a phone call and some flashing headlights ensured that a bear did not start a nuclear war.

CHAPTER 59

PETROV IN THE BUNKER

This is the natural counterpart to our last story. It is the tale of Stanislav Petrov, who saved the world.

By the 1980s the Soviet Union had built and launched a net of 'early-warning' satellites, designed to give Moscow the (slightly) advance knowledge that a nuclear attack was underway and to therefore allow a little time to react to it. A bunker near Moscow was that satellite network's control centre.

Stanislav Petrov, a Russian lieutenant colonel, was on duty in the bunker on 26 September 1983. A little after midnight, his centre's computer reported that an intercontinental ballistic missile had been fired by the USA at the USSR. As everything conventionally known about the doctrine of mutually assured destruction suggested that a first-strike nuclear attack by either side would mean the sudden launch of not one but *hundreds* of missiles simultaneously, Petrov simply didn't believe the system. The man thought the machine had malfunctioned.

But it wasn't his call to make. His supposed duty was clear: sound the alarm, Petrov – you are the spearpoint of our counterattack. You warn; we launch. That's how it's supposed to work.

But he ignored it.

Worse, the whizzbang new computer then reported four more missiles heading towards the USSR. Petrov wrote this off as an error *again*. In his defence, a little later ground radar showed no inbound missiles, neither one nor five, confirming his view. But the very point of the early-warning system was to give the Soviets a heads up before radar confirmation was possible – a heads up not meant to be stymied by the contrary views of one officer.

It seems that these false alarms were caused by an unusual alignment of sunlight bouncing from the tops of clouds and the satellites' orbits. Which would have seemed a daft reason to wipe out humanity, wouldn't it?

What happened to Petrov? Well, first off, no medal, that's for sure. They could have gone down that path, adopting and burnishing a cause for PR reasons – as we saw with the Georgians on the Texels in the incident known as the Night of the Bayonets in Chapter 6 – or on the other hand they could have sought to hush it up on grounds of national security. But too many people knew of the episode by the time such options were considered, and it was highly embarrassing that the new Soviet satellite system was second-guessed by a lowly officer – and, worse, second-guessed correctly. Even if that guessing prevented nuclear war.

So, it was a shuffle sideways, a little demotion, a nervous breakdown and early retirement. Such is often the fate for those who embarrass the institutions they serve by being correct. It's just that normally the fate of humanity doesn't hinge on them sticking to their guns.

Today's lesson, in a very different context, recalls that of Chapter 12's Portuguese consul who saved so many Jews in the Second World War… Sometimes, you are definitely going to be punished for doing what you know to be the right thing. You should still do it.

The tricky part which clouds this lesson is obvious. What if he'd been wrong…?

CHAPTER 60

REMEMBER THE SPARTANS

The ancient Greeks of course gave us the Olympic Games – a notion produced and fostered in one of those rare times in which they weren't battling against their hated war-to-the-knife rivals, the ancient Greeks.

Legend has it that one day at the Games, an elderly man was slowly making his way around the stadium, trying and failing to find a seat. His doddery progress was jeered by the crowd until he reached the stand taken by the Spartans.

As one, every Spartan stood up and offered up their place – including those older than the man himself.

The crowd were silenced by this, and then applauded.

The man turned to those nearest to him and said, 'All Greeks know the right thing to do, but only the Spartans do it.'

CHAPTER 61

LA SAGESSE NORMANDE

I am, from time to time, accused of being an arch-Eurosceptic. Which is fair. So I share this story from the former Labour MEP (and arch-Remainer) Richard Corbett.

The European Parliament, which by the way cannot initiate legislation, was in the depths of deep dispute. The debate was about the Gulf War but the details don't really matter. To the rescue rode a French MEP from the north of his fine country. He explained that his proposed compromise was thanks to '*la sagesse Normande*'.

This translates as being 'the wisdom of those from Normandy'; but (and I do not suggest inaccuracy here, to be clear) those interpreting his speech into English rendered this to those listening on the floor of the European Parliament as being 'thanks to Norman Wisdom'.

The speaker's surprise at the reaction as he held forth on this important subject can be imagined. Behold a moment that united Britain's warring MEPs across party lines.*

---

* Sadly, despite the famous extent to which this performer's Cold War fame extended to Eastern Europe (where thanks to his struggles on the silver screen as a little man against the system, he was one of the few Western actors whose movies were allowed to be aired, resulting in wildly more popular status there than in his home country and in him being an honorary citizen of Tirana), the enjoyment of this moment did not extend to the new 'accession country' members of the EU because Wisdom was known in the east as Mr Pitkin, one of his characters, not as Norman Wisdom.

Labour, Conservative, UKIP, SNP, Green... No other nationality quite understood why the British and Irish delegations promptly fell about laughing.

CHAPTER 62

BROADSWORDS. IN A PIT.

Anyone who's seen *Hamilton* – has anyone not by now? – knows that America's Founding Fathers went in for a bit of duelling from time to time, to the clear and unambiguous loss of the political talent pool. What some may not know is that this tendency lasted for quite some time – and even extended to Abraham Lincoln.

The closure of the Illinois* State Bank in 1842 put many holding its notes in jeopardy. Tempers were running high. The state auditor, James Shields, defended the decision. A fiery 'prairie lawyer', one Abraham Lincoln, attacked it, under a (soon revealed) pseudonym.

Lincoln's attacks were personal; Shields got on his high horse; Lincoln demanded he be more civil; Shields didn't back down; and before you knew it Shields called out the future President. The fight was to be in Missouri, where duelling was still legal.

As he was the one challenged, Lincoln got to choose weapons and the place in which the duel would be fought. Thus giving us one of history's great replies: 'Broadswords. In a pit.' I mean, the phrase itself is electrifying, isn't it?

Lincoln explained later that he felt sure Shields would

---

* Lincoln's home state.

kill him if pistols were used. As he was not keen on being killed, or on killing Shields either, he chose large, heavy swords so as to disarm his smaller opponent before the fight really got going. Shields accepted these terms and half of Illinois decamped to Missouri for the fight of the decade.

Lincoln was 6ft 4in.; Shields was 5ft 9in. Lincoln had noticeably long arms even for a tall man. As they entered the arena, Lincoln held out his sword and whacked a tree branch with it. The whirling blade, when combined with Lincoln's superior height and reach, showed that Shields wasn't really going to get near him, and the branch cleft in twain showed Lincoln's remarkable strength.

Gosh, do you know what, Shields thought, I'm not so sure about this duel business after all. On reflection, the men called a truce.

Lincoln, a man always deeply committed to honesty, never denied the truthfulness of the duelling episode – but he hated to talk about it. I like to think that he thought the whole thing rather dishonourable and certainly not to be admired – a good attitude to have had. Later, in the Civil War, Shields acquitted himself admirably as a leader of fighting men, and Lincoln – as President, of course – nominated Shields for a promotion. Any remaining rift between the two men was mended by duty.

Thank goodness Lincoln had the choice of weapons and chose so well. Otherwise, the history of his country might have been very different, and we might have had one more obscure subject of a musical instead of a President who fought for and reunited his country in the depths of its darkest hour.

CHAPTER 63

THE MOST UNUSUAL
DIPLOMATIC LETTER

Philip Deane (no relation, as far as I know) was *The Observer*'s man in Korea at the outset of their civil war. He was taken prisoner by the North Koreans whilst reporting on the front line.* His memoirs of that time, *I was a Captive in Korea*, are gripping and later gained attention as one of his fellow captives, MI6 officer George Blake, defected to the Russians via their Korean communist allies and, as the British did not know this for some decades to come, went on to betray his country from within the secret intelligence service many times over.

Prisoners taken by the North Koreans – civilians included – were treated very badly. Deane had taken several bullets to the leg during the episode that resulted in his capture, and his wounds were left untreated for some time. Deane was interned with other civilians – Americans, French and others – in an old school in a remote location. But he was taken into Pyongyang (full of promises of rewards and release) in an attempt to get him to broadcast propaganda for the regime. He didn't.

---

* Also known as Philippe Gigantès, Deane had a remarkable career after the war, serving as a senator in Canada and a minister in Greece.

Whilst he was in town, his captors received representations about him from the British authorities and others, and finally became convinced that he was genuinely a journalist rather than the spy they suspected (or pretended to suspect in order to heighten his fears and get him to broadcast). So, they treated his wounds at last, and he was kept for a while in a big house in Pyongyang. When the city was bombed by the UN, his captors would flee to bomb shelters, leaving him in the house. (They'd pretend to walk there slowly as if calm and untroubled but would sprint for the shelter as soon as they thought themselves to be out of sight: Deane could see them from windows.)

There were several broken radios lying around the house. During the regular 'bombing breaks' when he was separated from his captors, he found that by switching parts between the junked radios, he could get one of them to work. In this way he came to learn of the birth of Princess Anne, to the then Princess Elizabeth. He took this news back to the other interned civilians when he was finally returned to the school.

There, as they continued to be treated terribly, with some amongst their number even dying of starvation, the French diplomatic delegation imprisoned with him somehow obtained some paper (stolen from guards? The school? He never knew.).

Using home-made writing tools, they inscribed a formal letter of congratulations on the birth of Princess Anne to Vyvyan Holt, the British minister from the mission in Seoul, who was also interned with them. This story – of knowing the proper thing to do, of adhering to one's duty even if it might seem silly and far removed from one's circumstances, perhaps deriving some sense from it that there was still some sort of normality that yet survived, even with a knowing sense of absurdity and doing it despite the dangers the theft involved – touched me, so I share it with you.

Whilst others will of course hold different views on monarchy, I also find it striking to think that our link to a time so very greatly removed from our own is embodied in the lives of the royals featured in this anecdote; the same royals still serving our country today.

CHAPTER 64

AN AFTERNOON SPENT FISHING

King Abdullah II of Jordan is a great friend to the West. Sandhurst-trained,* his elite forces often participate in tough missions alongside Americans and Brits, and on some occasions he has not been averse to going along with them himself. But of course, before he was King, he was a prince, and his equally famous father King Hussein reigned.

On one occasion in the mid-1980s, in the course of attempts to maintain influence and to avoid bloodshed in the region, his father visited Iraq to try to talk sense into Saddam Hussein. Hindsight shows us that this was plainly an impossible task, but equally plainly it was one at which it was honourable to try. (This was also pretty broadminded, duty-orientated and pragmatic of King Hussein, as his first cousin, King Faisal II of Iraq, with whom he had been very close, had been overthrown and brutally executed by the Baathist movement that brought Saddam Hussein to power.)

As a gesture of goodwill, and because it was thought a good idea to train the heir in the art of diplomacy, Hussein took Abdullah, Abdullah's brother and two of his cousins

---

* Like his father and grandfather before him.

to Iraq with him. But what will we do whilst you're in talks with Saddam? asked Abdullah. Why, you'll spend time with his sons and help to ensure that the relationship is good from generation to generation! Well, not only did that future obviously, er, not happen; moreover Abdullah thought to himself, oh great. An afternoon with Uday and Qusay Hussein. Two of the world's most famous nutters. So, lads (I may paraphrase slightly) – what are we going to get up to today? Surprised, relieved, he was told, 'Fishing.'

Protestations that they didn't have any fishing outfits backfired when the entire junior Jordanian entourage was promptly issued with garish Hawaiian shirts for the occasion. Better stop complaining, lads – after all, it's only fishing; could have been a lot worse…

Well, they were out in a small motorboat on Lake Habbaniyah* before Abdullah realised something was missing. Where's the fishing kit, then?

From the footwell of the boat, Uday pulled out a big carrier bag full of… dynamite. Lots of dynamite. He started lighting sticks from the cigar he was puffing on. The first couple fizzled and were declared 'duds' – and thrown back into the footwell of the boat. This… is not sensible. As Abdullah and his cousin Talal, both military-trained, swiftly realised, these fuses could in fact still be burning. But could they tell the Husseins that they didn't know what they were doing and were in fact acting incredibly dangerously? No, they could not.

---

* In Anbar Province, west of Baghdad – quite some way west, requiring a flight to be taken. Plainly the Hussein brothers *really* liked fishing.

So, they pressed themselves to the rear of the boat as far as possible and crossed their fingers. The third stick lit, went over the side and went up in an enormous explosion. Ah, the serenity of a spot of fishing. Over the side went some amongst them to gather up some of the dead fish now floating on the surface.

Remarkably, nobody was killed in the course of this recreation, and Abdullah and his family returned home to Jordan unscathed and with some new memories.

Dynamite fishing with the Hussein brothers. What an afternoon.

CHAPTER 65

DECOMPRESSION

If you suffer from aviophobia, or, if you prefer, aerophobia – fear of flying, of course – please look away now. This is the story of British Airways Flight 5390.

On the morning of 10 June 1990, the BA flight from Birmingham to Málaga took off as normal. Eighty-seven souls were on board. Having executed their take-off without a hitch, the experienced crew in the cockpit of the plane, christened *The County of South Glamorgan*, took off their shoulder belts.

Then, the nightmare. The left side of the cockpit windscreen blew out. To state the obvious, this isn't supposed to happen; but it did.

Captain Tim Lancaster was propelled out the window by the decompression. Or rather, his top half was. His legs were caught on the flight control panel for a moment, allowing his colleagues to grab him by the legs. But most of him was still on the outside of the aircraft. His head banging repeatedly against the fuselage. The door of the cabin was blown in by the air. The autopilot was off, and the plane fell into a dive. The throttle was trapped by a combination of the door and Lancaster's legs, speeding the plane up. Loads of detritus from the main cabin was blown into the flight deck, which didn't help. His colleagues were hanging on to Lancaster for dear life. The plane was plummeting fast.

The announcement to take the brace position was made. I feel confident that on this occasion the passengers believed it. Alastair Atchison, the first officer, got the plane back on an even keel at a lower height and engaged the autopilot. The lower height part was important, as there wasn't enough oxygen aboard for everyone and Atchison needed to find an altitude with better air pressure to keep everyone alive. And, to state the obvious, he needed to land. He'd made a Mayday signal, but he didn't know if ground control was responding, given all the noise in the cockpit.

All the while, Captain Lancaster's head was bang-bang-banging on the side of the plane. Frankly, his colleagues – still hanging onto him – thought he was dead. His body was swiftly suffering from frostbite in the cold, quite apart from the repeated collisions with the airframe. Indeed, the cold was so bad that the stewards holding him got frostbite too. And they were exhausted. But on Atchison's instructions they kept hanging onto him – out of respect… and also because they didn't want him to go out of the window and into the engine.

Finally, they could hear ground control and were cleared to land at Southampton Airport, which seems fair – I don't think there were many aircraft with higher-priority needs at the time.

Oh, and by the way – Lancaster was in fact alive.

Atchison safely landed the plane with his captain

flapping around out the window, which is presumably a sight not often seen by the control tower. He had a couple of minor fractures, frostbite and, not surprisingly, shock. Otherwise, OK. He was back to flying in fewer than six months.

Crew members of the flight deservedly received medals for their conduct that day – the Queen's Commendation for Valuable Service in the Air. In addition, Atchison received the Polaris Award, the highest decoration available in civil aviation.

You'll be wondering why the window blew in. Well, air accident investigators did too. It turned out that when it was installed, most of the bolts used were too narrow, and those that weren't too narrow were too short. How reassuring! (There are two types of windscreen, this accident has forced me to learn. The first is the fitted-from-inside plug type, which is held in place by pressure. The second is the fitted-from-outside type, which is blown off by pressure. This was the latter.)

But accidents happen. That isn't the lesson from this story. Yes, the chances of them happening should be minimised; lessons should be learned in maintenance routines and manufacturing; where appropriate the negligent should be punished and so on.* I am sure that these things happened in the aftermath of Flight 5390. But whilst important, such things are the automatic results of any such incident.

---

* The aircraft returned to service and continued flying until 2001.

The lessons from this story are threefold, and they all come from Atchison. First: in a crisis, don't panic. Second: remember your training; you know what to do, if only you can remember lesson one. Third: don't give up on your colleagues. There may be more life in them than you think.

CHAPTER 66

TEMPORARY MEASURES

A reflection on a trio of temporary measures.

Value-added tax (VAT), which was introduced in 1973 when the UK joined the EEC, was the direct replacement of the purchase tax, which in turn was brought to us during the Second World War to reduce the wastage of materials during those challenging days.* Essentially the same tax as that brought to us in 1940 as a temporary measure, it is still adding 20 per cent to the price of goods bought in 2021 and is the government's third largest source of revenue today.†

Income tax has a yet more venerable temporary status.

---

* No discussion of VAT is complete without the ultimate digression: the Jaffa Cake tax case. Most food is 'zero-rated' for VAT but confectionary is bizarrely bifurcated into groups that are zero-rated and standard-rated. The logic is questionable. In any case, VAT is chargeable on chocolate (covered) *biscuits*, but not on chocolate (covered) *cakes*. The distinction is one of those 'boring but important' ones, at least if you care about situations in which a great deal of money is at stake. McVitie's, understandably, did. Their bestselling orange-flavoured product had been ruled to be a biscuit. This would mean a huge amount of cash going to HMRC. They claimed it was a cake. Whilst sold alongside biscuits and being biscuit-sized, they pointed out that the ingredients were much closer to that of a cake. It hardens when stale, like a cake, rather than softening when stale, like a biscuit. The VAT tribunal, asserting that the name itself was irrelevant, agreed. Whether they actually produced a giant Jaffa Cake to prove the point is unknown and may be a very popular urban legend (which your author wishes to be true, and he envies Donald Potter QC, who presided over the tax case of the century, the experience if it is). In any case, McVitie's won, rendering Jaffa Cakes immune from standard-rated VAT and saving the company – or the consumer – a great deal of state-imposed cost. That was back in 1991: consider all the Jaffa Cakes that have been eaten since then at a state-granted discount. And there was much rejoicing.

† After income tax and National Insurance.

Pitt the Younger introduced it in 1799 as a way to pay for arms in the Napoleonic Wars. Abandoned by Addington during the Peace of Amiens, reintroduced when fighting was back on again, cancelled again after Waterloo, then brought back in 1842 to deal with a 'temporary' problem in government cashflow, 'for three years'. I don't know about you, but to me it doesn't feel like we're funding French hostilities when the tax comes out of one's pay today, or bailing out the mid-nineteenth-century government of Robert Peel. And yet, here it still is.[*]

Pub licensing hours were restricted in the UK during the First World War to ensure that fighting men and manufacturing workers weren't too belted to defend the realm. Only very slightly liberalised after the war, the hours pretty much remained with us until the Licensing Act 2003 came into force in 2005.

Two lessons, both better put by others than by me. First, Milton Friedman: 'Nothing is so permanent as a temporary government programme.' Second, Benjamin Franklin: 'Those who would give up essential liberty to purchase a little temporary safety deserve neither liberty nor safety.' (He might have added: 'And will soon lose both.')

---

[*] Even when everyone agreed it should go, it didn't. Both sides in the 1874 general election pledged to repeal it. Disraeli won and reneged on the pledge, as Gladstone most likely would have done if he'd prevailed, too.

CHAPTER 67

THE FIGHTING DENTIST

Ben Salomon graduated with a degree in dentistry in 1937. He immediately applied to both the Canadian and US Armies – but was rejected from both. He therefore started a dental practice on the west coast and was soon thriving. So, of course, he was promptly drafted into the US Army as a private as war loomed.

By the time his abilities were recognised and the army commissioned him into the dental corps in 1942, this tough contrarian soul had settled into infantry life, and he tried in vain to stay with his machine-gun team.

Serving in the war in the Pacific, Salomon was promoted to captain and volunteered for the position of a surgeon, which had fallen vacant. Thus, when the Japanese attacks began on the Mariana Islands, he was running a field hospital mere yards behind the frontline. Things went badly for the Americans, and the Japanese attack began to overwhelm the line. He was treating a patient when prompted to take up arms by the sight of a Japanese soldier bayoneting the wounded some way off. Salomon picked up a rifle, killed him and went back to treating the wounded. But soon more came. Salomon was quickly engaged in hand-to-hand combat, dispatching four enemies. Then he picked up a machine gun. This was something he knew how to use... Refusing to abandon his post and his patients, Salomon mounted a rear-guard action, solo, to allow time for the hospital to be evacuated and his comrade patients saved.

The American forces fell back, then slowly retook the territory. When they recovered the hospital, some fifteen hours after he was left there alone, they found Salomon. His body had fallen over his gun at the last. Before him, the bodies of ninety-eight Japanese soldiers. Salomon was the only defender of the hospital. He had killed them all.

His body had seventy-six bullet wounds and many, many bayonet wounds. The attackers, when finally upon him, had unleashed a frenzied revenge on this bravest of men. Salomon was wrongly denied an award for his actions because of an incorrect interpretation of the rules regarding medics. Whilst no medical non-combatant can be awarded for actions during an *offensive*, Salomon's of course were not. Medics are permitted to use force in 'final defence' of themselves or their patients.

Thus in 1998, almost sixty years after his death, a second recommendation was made, and in 2002 his brave last stand was finally recognised as he deserved. He is a posthumous recipient of the Medal of Honor.*

---

* Fittingly, it was presented to the dental school at the University of Southern California, where he had studied. Whilst the original is now in the Army Medical Department Museum, a replica is on display at USC today.

CHAPTER 68

WHAT COMES AFTER A LEAP INTO FREEDOM?

A parlour game: who is your favourite defector? Of course, it's hard to look past Rudolph Nureyev or Czesław Miłosz or Miloš Forman. Gordievsky we already discussed in Chapter 21. Korchnoi in Chapter 25. Stalin's daughter's defection is a pretty eye-catching case. Moreover, Alexander Godunov was a successful ballet dancer who played one of the German terrorists in *Die Hard* after his defection, which is very hard to beat.

I find it impossible to pick, but I have no such doubts about my favourite *image* of a defector. So now we turn to the sad story of Konrad Schumann, the border guard who jumped the wire between East Germany and freedom in 1961, as the Berlin Wall was being built.

Schumann served in the 'BePo' – the Bereitschaft-spolizei – a paramilitary police organisation which was created to act as the boot by which the state would stamp down upon rebellion. Its officers were meant to be loyal beyond question. But Schumann's case served to show that, given the opportunity, some even amongst the enforcing class would prefer the West to the repression of their own harsh republic of watchers and informers.

Sent to guard the new barrier site – really, to keep people of the East in, I suppose; the duty of a generation of bullies to come – he was only nineteen that day in 1961. And, only three days after its construction had commenced, the Berlin 'Wall' in his section was only wire so far.

As he told it, whilst at his post he saw a young woman in the East pass a bouquet of flowers over the wire to an older woman in the West. It was obviously her mother. Who parts families like this? Who wishes to be a part of the regime that does it?

Thus, unnoticed by his comrades, Schumann had pressed down a part of the wire near him and passed word to a Westerner watching that he would jump. So, the Western police were ready to whisk him away from the scene in a car if he dared to follow through. He dared.

Standing guard by the low loops of barbed wire, his back against a stone wall, he was urged to come over by the crowd gathered on the Western side. 'Come over! Come over!' they cried.

Many such moments are lost in time like tears in rain. Justly or unjustly, what makes this one so remembered was the widespread presence of people with cameras that day, ensuring the episode was captured from so many different angles and in such detail. His leap for freedom gave the world one of the enduring images of the Cold War. Arms outstretched, his gun on his back, muzzle facing downward with the strap stretched tight in his hand, his head is down, determined, face all but unseen beneath the helmet. An everyman for those repressed in the East.

But after his great, impetuous moment, life in the West brought him little happiness. Relocated to Bavaria, far from the border, finding work, marrying and having a son – nevertheless he was full of regret and remorse and fear. Might he be targeted for retribution as so many other defectors and critics had been? Moreover, what would happen to his family in the East because of him and what he had done?

He said that he never truly felt free until the wall – that barrier so closely aligned with the barriers in his own life; the wall with which he was so inescapably associated – came down. But we can wait for decades thinking that some goal will be the vital thing that fixes everything, only to find bitter disappointment. He visited family. They were strangers to him. People who had known him before he 'deserted' them wanted nothing to do with him.

So, after the seemingly positive resolution of the conflict that had defined his life, after the peace for which he had waited for so long, there was no peace for him. He hanged himself from a tree in his orchard.

Without sounding too Scandinavian existentialist, the lesson here is bleak. We must all strive for happiness. Many will find it. But for others… well, some will never be happy without freedom. Others will never be happy away from their homeland. Some, sad to say, will never be happy at all.

But there is an irony which makes this story revealing. For as Schumann's story shows us, these unhappy souls can still provide us with glorious, soaring moments which serve both to inspire and to bring hope to a generation to come – and to those on both sides of a wall or a wire.

CHAPTER 69

BATTING ON

This is a story about cricket and courage. It is the story of the Kiwi innings against South Africa in Johannesburg in 1953–54.

New Zealand did not have a single win from the twenty-seven Tests they had played to date, so things weren't looking super for the visiting side. True to this run of form, the opening Test saw the tour begin with an innings defeat in Durban. Most did not hold out much hope for the Kiwis in the second Test, which began on Christmas Eve in Johannesburg.

But New Zealand surprised their hosts, with great bowling leaving SA on 259 for eight as play that Christmas Eve drew to a close. The happiness brought by success on the pitch did not last long. For Boxing Day brought news of the Tangiwai disaster. A railway bridge on the Whangaehu river on New Zealand's North Island had collapsed, sending a locomotive and half a dozen passenger carriages into the river. Some 151 people died.[*] One of them was the fiancée of the leading NZ bowler, Bob Blair.

---

[*] It remains New Zealand's worst rail accident to date.

Blair withdrew from the match in grief, and more broadly the morale of the visiting side was shattered. They sought to rally themselves but no doubt the very notion of playing a game after what had happened seemed strange to them. I imagine that in the modern age it would have been called off.

South Africa's tail end was swiftly dispatched – but so were the Kiwi openers. Ferocious fast bowler Neil Adcock was in aggressive form for SA, and soon the Kiwis were nine for two. Bert Sutcliffe went in to bat for NZ – and was soon the third Kiwi to be hit by Adcock's bodyline bowling. The third ball Adcock played struck him in the head, knocking him out. He was taken off covered in blood and taken to hospital. (Remember, helmets weren't that common until the 1970s…)

John Reid came next and was hit five times by Adcock. Lawrie Miller was hit badly and followed Sutcliffe to hospital. Sport, or massacre? Fifty-seven for five at lunch; two men in hospital and one stricken with grief.

Miller, against medical advice and in an act that would definitely not be allowed in any modern sporting environment, resumed his innings after lunch. But he was soon bowled, and the follow-on loomed.* Weak batsmen remained in the order. The Kiwis had had it, it seemed.

Cue Sutcliffe, head wrapped in bandages and unsteady on his feet, emerging from the pavilion. To a man, the

---

* The bowling side can force the batting side to immediately play their second batting innings if the score of their first is low enough. It's not a good thing.

crowd applauded wildly at the gesture. What a sight it must have been. He wasn't going to be doing much running. So… he slogged. Wham. Wham. Like a volunteer vaccinating and dispatching locked-down patients, he thumped out six after six from the off and saw off the risk of the follow-on.

But he ran out of partners. SA's Ironside had massacred those batting with him when Sutcliffe didn't have the strike. When the last of them fell, everyone started off towards the pavilion. When out came Bob Blair.

Grief-stricken though he was, when Blair was told about his team's plight, he came to help. The bandaged Sutcliffe went to meet him in a silenced ground, and they walked to the middle together, arm in arm. I tear up thinking about that pair on that walk. Those in the ground are said to have felt the same. If that walk to the centre in a silent arena doesn't get you, try this: cricket writer Dick Brittenden wrote, 'Before he faced his first ball, Blair passed his glove across his eyes in the heart-wringing gesture of any small boy, anywhere; in trouble but defiant.' Gulp.

Sutcliffe promptly hit three sixes in an over, and plucky Blair added one, too (his only scoring shot). As it happens, those shots went into the stand behind long-on – the only area allowed for black spectators during Apartheid. They always supported the visitors and went crazy for each six.

Blair left the scorer largely untroubled, but his presence let Sutcliffe make a serious difference to the innings.

Eventually Blair was bowled, leaving Sutcliffe unbeaten on eighty.

The follow-on was avoided. And in the end New Zealand lost. But that's not really the point, is it? At the end of that remarkable innings, Sutcliffe and Blair walked together from that crease, arm in arm once again, and into sporting immortality.

CHAPTER 70

THE ARC LIGHT FLIGHT

David Donovan's raw and powerful book *Once a Warrior King* is no doubt very unfashionable these days, setting out as it does the work he and brave men like him undertook against the Vietcong. Small, highly trained specialist units like his were embedded with anti-communist Vietnamese forces in a fashion that was the very antithesis of the drafted mass movement of men – and far more successful. Modern critics would no doubt label this 'white saviour' activity and the like.

Donovan lived and fought alongside his Vietnamese brethren in a remote part of the Mekong Delta. One of their missions was disrupting the supply chain between the North Vietnamese Army (NVA) and their affiliated units operating over the border in Cambodia. The time came when a big NVA push was looming. Intelligence confirmed it. Donovan feared that soon two regiments of hostile soldiers would be rolling over his little mud fort, which was manned by him, four other Americans and a single platoon of local militia.

Late one night, a reconnaissance plane confirmed that the enemy was coming downriver. Over a thousand lights could be seen. Donovan called for help. He asked for an F4 fighter bomber attack. None could be tasked. He asked for a helicopter gunship attack. None was available. He sat numbly before his radio, in silence punctuated only by static. The silence that meant he would die. I think of him in the Delta at that moment, and of the man on the other end of the radio who knew what it meant too.

The faraway voice then spoke to Donovan unprompted. How would you like Arc Light [i.e. a B-52 strike]? I think we might be able to swing that.

Good Lord. A B-52 bombing run on regiments of the enemy who are aboard a flotilla of sampans and closing in on my isolated position? Why, yes. Yes please – that sounds just the ticket.

Quite the escalation, this. It's like being told that you can't have a knife or a gun but your backup will use the atomic bomb for you. Usually one doesn't use a sledge-hammer to crack a nut, but if it's the only option available to you…

Arc Light was approved.

Donovan went to tell the local village boss what was happening. Then they waited in the still night.

They never heard the planes. Neither did their victims. Suddenly the sky lit up like midday, and the ground shook with fury. It was over in thirty seconds. Perhaps one plane had been diverted from other duties to help out; perhaps two. It was a limited strike. But what a strike it was. The whole thing had taken less than an hour, from the plaintive request for help over the radio to the visitation of nemesis upon the river.

Donovan and his men went to the strike zone at first

light. Nothing bigger than matchstick-style splinters remained of hundreds of boats. Almost no equipment. Evidence of great human suffering but almost no sign of victims. The survivors had obviously collected the dead and limped back over the border.

Reflect again on that moment over the radio. Diverting a B-52 bombing raid is not something generally volunteered per se. But moreover, why were B-52s so readily available at such short notice and in that place? Donovan does not say, but I think that one can tell. This was, I think, confirmation that the USA was bombing Cambodia. Now, it is known. Then, it was secret. Such a thing would have been tightly guarded, not to be disclosed. But it was.

Donovan's life was saved by someone he had never met, and never would meet, breaking the rules.

CHAPTER 71

REAGAN AND THE AIR
TRAFFIC CONTROLLERS

This is the story of Ronald Reagan's confrontation with a powerful union: the Professional Air Traffic Controllers Organization (PATCO).

PATCO had been militating about pay and conditions for some time. Before the 1980 election, the Reagan campaign had indicated support for some of their concerns. This may have given them greater hopes about the prospect of their demands being met under Reagan than under Carter. If so, they were wrong.

In 1981, the new Reagan administration offered the air traffic controllers a package of pay increases and enhanced benefits that would have seen them become better paid than their private-sector counterparts. The offer was refused. The air traffic controllers must have thought that the government simply could not cope without them and that the withdrawal of their labours would produce paralysis that an administration could not bear. There are later echoes of this in the UK with regard to our train drivers, of course.

PATCO lost in court and were ordered to return to work. Over 11,000 of them refused. So, President Reagan dismissed them all.* Rather than the system falling over, positions were plugged with supervisors, transferred personnel and military operators.

In indicating that a government will not be held to ransom, there is an important message here. Confronted by recalcitrant and powerful miners, Edward Heath asked at a snap general election, 'Who runs Britain?' In his case, the electorate's answer was resoundingly 'not you', but still, the thrust of the question is right.

The lesson here isn't merely about strength. It's about preparation. If you intend to force someone to work, the law must be on your side and you must have an alternative available; if you are going to have your bluff called, you must be ready.

Whether the workers be, say, air traffic controllers you wish to work for less money than they demand, or those undertaking hard and poorly paid work in nursing homes whom you wish to compulsorily vaccinate at risk of their positions, you've got to have a backup plan if they say no.

---

* He also banned them from working in federal positions for the rest of their lives, which seems rather spiteful.

CHAPTER 72

THE FORGOTTEN FAIRFAX

This is the story of a man who fought for, and then against, and then for, the monarchy.

Thomas Fairfax was born to Yorkshire gentry.[*] He learned his army trade fighting for the Protestants in Holland, and then served his King, Charles I, in command of a cavalry against the Scots. Keen to avoid conflict between Crown and Parliament, he sought compromise in the crisis of 1641–42. But when push came to shove and war came, he was for Parliament.

Fairfax and his family led parliamentary supporters in the north, fighting significant royalist forces for over a year, thus preventing them from marching into the southern shires to help Charles. With his father acting as general of the parliamentary forces in the north, Fairfax Junior continued to lead his troops in person, winning the Battles of Winceby, Nantwich and Selby at the head of his cavalry (and was routed at Marston Moor, where his brother fell in battle, but we shall overlook this). He survived several injuries in the course of these fights for the future of his country.

Still in his early thirties, he was made commander of the

---

[*] The line exists to this day, with the peerage presently held by the 14th Lord Fairfax.

New Model Army and won the crucial Battle of Naseby, smashed the last royalist army at Langport and then took Oxford, now best known as home to a second-rate university but then, in 1646, the royalist capital.[*]

When the war was over, as history well attests, Fairfax was overlooked in favour of Oliver Cromwell, to the extent that whilst the name of his rival in leadership is now (in)famous, that of Fairfax is largely forgotten. Harsh for one recognised even by Charles I[†] to be a man of honour.

Unlike most of the parliamentary leadership, Fairfax thought victory ought not to be followed by vengeance. He refused to take part in Charles I's trial, didn't attend it and argued against his execution. When Cromwell invaded Ireland he stayed at home, and he declined to lead the invasion of Scotland. These principled stands meant that Fairfax, once at the very forefront of the parliamentary movement, was gradually sidelined (by dint of his own choices) into semi-obscurity.

But at this most important period of conflict in determining what Britain would become, the tide of history was not finished with Fairfax. For Fairfax had seen the revolution as a means to a better country – rather than envisaging the military rule to which it gave rise as constituting the outcome for Britain in perpetuity. Thus, having given up his parliamentary command, in time he raised troops in Yorkshire and fought the parliamentarians.

---

[*] In the latter battle, Fairfax, a rather gentle warrior given to writing poetry, sought to save the libraries from being pillaged.

[†] Fairfax had charge of the King as a prisoner for some time.

Once again, he tied up important military resources in the north, preventing them from reinforcing an embattled leadership in the south. But this time it was for the Crown and against the parliamentary army. Thus, thanks in large part to forgotten Fairfax, restorationist forces were able to march to restore King Charles II.*

Whilst he enjoyed a decade of rest at his family seat in Yorkshire at the end of his life, there is no doubt that these repeated calls to duty took their toll. The lesson here is that neither moderation nor reasonableness, neither determination nor bravery, mean one can avoid taking sides. Neither does it mean that one can win victories that prevent further conflict. Rather, sometimes, having these qualities and being true to one's beliefs mean one must fight on both sides, and fight and fight again.

---

* It must be said that this change of heart, along with his universally acknowledged honourable behaviour on the battlefield, ensured that he escaped the kind of punishment visited upon most leaders of the revolution.

CHAPTER 73

LAZOWSKI'S PRIVATE WAR

Eugene Lazowski* was a doctor in German-occupied Poland – and a very brave one. He escaped a prisoner-of-war camp and returned to his home town of Rozwadów† to work for the Polish Red Cross. His garden was set directly against the fence that enclosed the Jewish ghetto. Whilst Polish doctors were absolutely not allowed to treat the Jews, and the death penalty applied to Poles who helped Jews during the Holocaust, he knew that his duty to these most vulnerable people in awful conditions meant that he should somehow try.

A system emerged. When a prisoner of the ghetto became unwell, a rag would be tied to Lazowski's fence. Remarkably, he would then break *into* the ghetto under cover of darkness, taking medicine to those who needed it and treating patients in rudimentary, makeshift moving medical facilities.

Of course, this created a problem. Pharmacies and surgeries keep records, and in this time of madness none of these people in dire need were meant to be his patients. So, he systematically exaggerated and fabricated the records

---

* Charmingly, having been born in the United States, Lazowski was named after his birthplace: Eugene, Oregon. He returned towards the end of his life and passed away in his namesake town.
† Now a district of Stalowa Wola, south-east Poland.

kept in his registers of medicine given to non-Jewish patients. (He was helped by the fact that he was responsible for treating those passing through a railway station nearby, rendering some of these details all but impossible to check if anyone had a mind to do so.)

But he went yet further. The Nazis were terrified of germs. The Master Race particularly feared typhus, which had spread like wildfire in the trenches of the First World War. This, Lazowski realised, was potentially to his – and the Jews' – advantage.

Medical practitioners were obliged to report all possible typhus cases to the German authorities and dispatch samples of blood to be tested in laboratories run by them. The outcomes for confirmed cases were grimly bifurcated. Non-Jews with typhus were put into quarantine (and avoided detention in labour camps, to avoid outbreaks there); Jews with typhus were executed. But still, Lazowski realised, the existence of such procedures could be used to help those in the ghetto. If enough cases arose in a particular area, an epidemic would be declared. The Germans would understandably seek to avoid regions so designated – allowing the population to live their lives with interference from the Nazis running at a fraction of that seen in the rest of Poland.

Lazowski realised that the Weil–Felix test used to detect typhus could be 'tricked'. Inject someone with dead bacteria and it would create antibodies in their blood, which on testing would yield a false positive result for typhus.

So, unbelievably, he started whacking dead bacteria into

the blood of basically anyone who came his way. Got a cough? A rash? Here, have some dead bacteria in your arm. Now, we'd better send your blood off for some tests. Whoops, what's this? TYPHUS?!

Which might give us pause. This isn't completely clear-cut, is it? Let's note that he didn't tell his patients what was going on when he injected them on a false premise with something that, at the very least, they didn't need. But a war was on and genocide was looming. Let's also note that those so injected weren't actually made sick by this.

By this point Lazowski had a partner in his deception: Stanisław Matulewicz, another doctor. They spoofed the system carefully, producing more false positives in winter when genuine typhus would be more prevalent. They even referred some of those they'd injected with dead antibodies to other doctors, who would dutifully go on to report the fake typhus cases themselves. Soon the case count rose to the point that their region was declared an 'epidemic area' – and tada, no Nazis.

The Germans were many things, but they weren't dumb, and they couldn't help but notice that it seemed that nobody in town was actually dying. They sent a team to Rozwadów to check things out. But Lazowski was ready for them. He got together the sickest-looking people in town (who had been injected with the harmless bacteria of course) and put them in a particularly slummy building. One look at this set-up and the Nazi delegates no doubt thought to themselves, 'We'd rather be somewhere else, please.' A couple of tests were administered, which of course proved positive, and they promptly hightailed it.

Lazowski and Matulewicz saved, on a rough estimate, 8,000 people with this safe haven from the Germans over three years of occupation, all with a harmless bacteria injection.

Lesson: if you're brave enough, all manner of ways exist to fight oppression. And not all involve fighting.

CHAPTER 74

OPERATION SOURCE

It's been a while since we've had a tale of naval derring-do. So – have a tot of rum and tuck yourselves in for the tale of Operation Source.

The German battleship *Tirpitz* was the pride of the *Kriegsmarine*. Some 2,000 tons heavier than her sister ship *Bismarck* thanks to wartime adaptations made after she was launched, she was the heaviest battleship ever built by a European navy at the time[*] and was the subject of totemic pride in the Nazi war machine. Indeed, such was her status that Hitler's repeated personal interventions partially stymied her effectiveness. The Führer insisted that she not be exposed to danger (which plainly rather defeats the point of a battleship), especially from aircraft carriers.

This meant that she was deployed less often, and less effectively, than German naval commanders would have wished. Nevertheless, she was a powerful presence in the calculations made by both sides in the deadly fencing and probing, as the Allies sought to bring materiel to Russia via the Atlantic convoys and the Germans sought to prevent them.

---

[*]   Later (just) surpassed by HMS *Vanguard*.

A 'fleet in being' is a naval force of such significance that even whilst in port she changes enemy plans, tying up ships that might otherwise be fruitfully deployed elsewhere in guarding against the risk of her sailing and changing the balance of power in the arena. Such was the *Tirpitz*.

All in all, the Allies needed to get at her. Britain tried to bomb her several times but defences were strong in the Norwegian ports, and all that we had to show for our efforts were lost Halifax bombers. So, necessity – especially in war – being the mother of invention, we turned to a new capability: midget submarines.

You had to be brave as hell to get into one of these things. If something – anything – went wrong, you were all but guaranteed to be done for. Circa 50ft long, X-class midget submarines were towed behind normal submarines until they reached the area in which they would be deployed. Crews – three, or later four, men* – would then be transferred to them by dinghy.

The British planned to use six midget submarines against the *Tirpitz* and other German ships berthed with her – but two sank on the way, one with the loss of the crew that had just been transferred to it, underscoring the point about the dangers they posed and the requirement for great bravery. Let us take a moment to reflect on the deaths of those men, no less brave than their comrades who continued on to take on the *Tirpitz*. They gave their

---

* A diver was added to the crew of commander, pilot and engineer as the submarine's capabilities became better understood.

lives in the service of their country, dying in a tiny tin can off the coast of Norway, largely unremembered. *Vale.*

So it was that in the end only four midget submarines went in to the harbour at Kåfjord under the cover of darkness that September evening in 1943.

One X-class soon developed mechanical problems and had to turn back, so we were down to three. This wasn't as bad as it might have been as, unbeknownst to the Brits, the *Scharnhorst* was out on exercises, reducing our potential target list in the harbour.

Midget or not, the ships were spotted. One was promptly sunk by the *Tirpitz*'s guns. So now two remained. Both successfully placed their charges under the *Tirpitz*. But both were fired upon and were unable to escape. Both crews, remarkably, survived and were captured by the Germans – and very soon after these brave sailors were in German hands, their work bore fruit. Explosions tore through the *Tirpitz*, causing her to take on over 1,000 tons of water and list in the harbour. Much of her machinery and weaponry were damaged.

Repairs to the *Tirpitz* took more than six months, and not long after that she was finally sunk by Lancaster bombers.* The work of a few men in tiny submersibles had crippled the pride of the German fleet for long enough to ensure that she played no meaningful part in the war before her end.†

---

* By the time she was sunk, the Allies had lost thirty-eight aircraft in attacks on her – underscoring the significant success of the X-class attack.

† Journalist Ludovic Kennedy wrote that 'she lived an invalid's life and died a cripple's death'.

The commanders of both the successful X-class ships received the Victoria Cross. Bravo, Lieutenants Donald Cameron (aged twenty-seven) and Basil Place (aged twenty-two), and your gallant crews.

CHAPTER 75

WHAT IF THE CHICKENS AREN'T HUNGRY?

The least interesting thing about the Battle of Drepanum (nowadays Trapani in Sicily) is what happened at the Battle of Drepanum. The more interesting parts are what came before and after. In sum. Rome v Carthage. First Punic War. Rome had consolidated control of mainland Italy and (historically not their strong point) had been notching up victories at sea. They were keen to carry on doing so. Thus rose and fell Publius Claudius Pulcher, for whom things were going well until they weren't. (Pulcher, by the way, means 'handsome'. Not for the first or last time, it seems that the public may have been swayed by a leader's matinée idol good looks into entrusting them with responsibilities for which hindsight shows they were less than ideally equipped.)

PCP took a Roman fleet up a channel at Drepanum, seeking to ambush the Carthaginians at night whilst they were at anchor. But the Punic admiral was ahead of him, putting to sea via another channel, and in open waters they utterly marmalised the Romans. PCP's fleet lost over ninety ships and (gulp) 20,000 men.

This wasn't good. But it was war, and people realised that in war, losses happen. The bigger problem for PCP was that he had ignored the chickens. No, that isn't a typo. The sacred chickens of Rome had refused to eat before the battle. This was a bad omen in the eyes of those who gave credence to such things. PCP was not such a one: throw them into the sea, he said. If they won't eat, let them drink!

Bold. And had the battle gone his way then not only would this affront have been forgiven; it might have redefined attitudes towards omens and the like thereafter, and PCP would have been seen as a visionary. But it didn't, so it didn't, and he wasn't. Instead, he returned to disgrace. Wasn't it obvious that this would go badly, given the omens? Weren't you warned? His friends and family had to beg for leniency for him, and he sort of got it – a whopping fine was levied upon him, but he avoided execution.

But his name was stained for ever by the chickens, and his family would struggle to make progress whilst that stain was extant – especially his son, who was a promising politician and fighter in his own right. What can a man do when once shown the heights of leadership and glory but now reduced to the depths of shame and disgrace, seemingly a burden to those he loves? Some mount comebacks, even from setbacks greater than this. Others don't. PCP was one of the latter. He died soon after he escaped real punishment – probably by his own hand.

Lesson: you may very well be right in thinking the views of others superstitious nonsense. But it's probably best not to be rude about it – especially as we all make mistakes, and as you may make a whopper yourself, it follows that one day you may need those superstitious nonsense-spouters on your side.

CHAPTER 76

THE LION OF AFRICA

This is the story of a man who led a force of 14,000 against 300,000, successfully, for four years. It is the story of Paul von Lettow-Vorbeck, the Lion of Africa.

Lettow-Vorbeck's memoirs give us a glimpse of encounters with famous figures in his early years, such as the great military strategist von Moltke, who was famously supposed to have laughed only twice in his life: once when told a particular French fortress was absolutely impregnable, and once when informed that his mother-in-law had died. Lettow-Vorbeck was a man of significant personal bravery. He was posted to German colonies in what is now Namibia at the start of the twentieth century, and fighting there left him permanently blind in one eye. It was this fighting that taught him much about what we now call guerrilla warfare.

When the First World War came, he found himself commanding German forces in East Africa. His command of *Schutztruppe* was tiny – some 5,000 men, half German volunteer officers and non-commissioned officers; half indigenous troops ('Askaris'). There was some talk of east Africa being declared neutral in the conflict (in the nineteenth century, the Great Powers contemplated colonies remaining inviolate during European conflicts). Given his situation this might have been thought attractive, but Lettow-Vorbeck was having none of that.

Instead, he battled the Allies wherever he could find them. He found himself facing an array of Belgian, British, Indian and Portuguese forces much larger than his own. He fought the lot. He fought pitched battles, such as the Battle of Tanga, in which he repulsed a British expeditionary force, and the Battle of Jassin, where the British surrendered to him and were treated with decency and released on their way upon a promise to play no further part in the war. He mounted lightning raids into British colonial territory in what is now Kenya and Uganda. He took naval guns from a scuttled ship and used them in the field.

His forces grew (to 14,000 at its height) as men of the region, drawn to this strong man who spoke to them as his fellow warriors in fluent Swahili, came to fight for Imperial Germany – or, more truthfully, for Lettow-Vorbeck.

He knew that his theatre of war would never be central to the conflict's outcome. His aim was therefore to make the Allies commit as many troops as possible to the fight against him, thus depriving them of resources that might otherwise be more fruitfully committed – or not, given the profligate nature of war in the European theatre – to the Western Front. As time went on, he continued to accumulate victories, but circumstances were harder and harder. Forever faced by superior numbers, deprived of support and materiel from Germany by a successful British blockade, his men fought on using weapons they captured from those they defeated.

Deprived of real bases, they worked as a mobile army, living off the land. Supplies dwindled. Rations were cut. They fought on. In other such environments, colonial subjects would have deserted the banner. After all, what did they owe to a far-off land? Lettow-Vorbeck's Askaris did not. For, as I have implied, they didn't really fight for Germany at all; they fought for him.

As usual, there is more than one side to a story. Awful things are done in war. The tactics required to keep the men commanded by Lettow-Vorbeck a viable fighting force led to deprivation and starvation for the civilian populations amongst whom they moved. Lettow-Vorbeck remained undefeated at the end of the war. Moreover, towards its conclusion he had actually taken several British towns – the only German so to do in the entire conflict. He surrendered after the Armistice by agreement on his own terms. Indeed, because of the time news of the Armistice took to reach their region, Lettow-Vorbeck's troops were the last men fighting the First World War and fired its last shots. When they finally surrendered, it was wryly realised by their new captors that almost all the weaponry had been taken from British forces they'd defeated.

Lettow-Vorbeck strove to secure early release from prisoner status for his brave soldiers. When he was separated from them by the Allies, to a man his Askaris formed up into ranks in the prisoner-of-war camp and cried out to be allowed to follow him.

In later life, he went into politics but did not thrive as, greatly to his credit of course, he opposed Hitler – just one more reason to like him.* His sons and his son-in-law all died fighting for Germany in the Second World War. He died in Germany in his ninety-fourth year, remaining to the last an example of the lost German dream and, with all its faults no doubt, the different history his country and its people at home and abroad might have lived but for Nazism.

---

* Offered an important ambassadorship under Hitler, he told the Führer – forgive this, readers – to go fuck himself.

CHAPTER 77

NON-STOP

This is the story of L 59, which undertook the longest non-stop military airship flight ever – over a hundred years ago.

In our last story, we saw how a combination of distance from home and a successful British blockade made re-supplying Paul von Lettow-Vorbeck, the Lion of Africa, all but impossible in the First World War. But that did not mean that Germany didn't try. Friedrichshafen has always been the home of the Zeppelin. Today perhaps best known by skiers using its little airport for package tours, the pretty town on Lake Constance was essentially flattened by the Allies in the Second World War.

But in the First World War, it was the southernmost hub for a flight from Germany southwards – which, given the nature of the conflict, was uncommon.

Lettow-Vorbeck's *Schutztruppe* were hanging on against the odds in east Africa and Germany was meant to deliver them one mega-supply to keep them going. Thus, L 59, a Zeppelin, left Friedrichshafen one day in November 1917 for a one-way trip to German east Africa.

Even with a stop at Jamboli in Bulgaria, the last friendly airfield before 2,000 miles of ocean and Entente-held territory, the flight was ominously challenging. There would be no chance to refuel at the other end, so the plan was always for the Zeppelin to get to the German colony and never fly again. Instead of returning, all her parts would be used by Lettow-Vorbeck's forces, and her crew would join his miniature army. Her balloon would become tents. Her framework would become radio towers. She carried a good deal of materiel and food, and a medical team keenly needed by the *Schutztruppe*.

After taking off from Jamboli, she raced south across the Mediterranean. She weathered dangerous electrical storms over Crete. She experienced mechanical difficulties over the Nile. She lost power. Then, a near-disaster. Rising heat from the desert reduced her buoyancy. A crash was just averted.

She flew on. Her brave crew endured boiling heat in the day and freezing temperatures at night. They were exhausted. Their exposure and tiredness led to headaches – and even hallucinations. One tries to imagine that moment, suspended from a balloon filled with explosive gas, tired beyond measure, thousands of miles from anyone on your side, when a man realises that those around him upon whom he depends for survival have started seeing things. I think that this can fairly be described as a low moment. Yet her comrades needed her. She flew on.[*]

Alas, over 2,000 miles into her epic journey, the L 59 was ordered to turn around. Lettow-Vorbeck had failed to hold the target zone for landing and there was no safe area

---

[*] By the way, most sources refer to a Zeppelin as 'it'. This didn't seem right to me. But trust me, searching online for whether a Zeppelin is a he or a she yields results rather different to those for which one was searching. I've just gone with 'she'.

in which she might put down. All that he could offer was
the chance of mountainous territory that seemed almost
guaranteed to end in disaster for a Zeppelin. Conscious-
ly refusing his only chance of support from home must
have been so hard for Lettow-Vorbeck – but the prospects
of landing without it all going wrong just weren't good
enough. The L 59's crew was devastated. They begged to be
allowed to go on.

Instead, having already been in the air for almost a hundred hours, they had to turn about and go all the way back
to Jamboli, experiencing all the tribulations they'd already
gone through once again. They made it with a couple
of days of fuel left, their achievement and their bravery
not lessened in my eyes by the stymying of their mission
through no fault of their own.

Sad to say, the L 59 met with an ignominious end. Deprived despite her crew's gallantry of the destiny that was
the completion of the *Schutztruppe* resupply, she was a
vessel without a purpose, it seemed. Officers cast around
for something to do with her. In the end, she set off to
bomb the British in Malta. For reasons for ever to remain
unknown, she exploded in mid-air, crashing into the ocean
with the loss of all hands.

She was undone by cause or causes unknown rather
than by hostile act: her enemies never touched her. Her
4,200-mile flight remains the non-stop military airship
record to this day.

CHAPTER 78

GOODBYE, BOYS

This is the story of the Halifax Pier – but not the last of Barrett's privateers.

One cold morning in December 1917, Vince Coleman was at work at the Richmond railway station in Halifax, Canada. It was not long until he let himself be blown up.

Coleman worked at a true transport nexus. The main railway line to Halifax passed close to his post, where he dispatched trains; the busy harbour at Halifax was a few hundred feet away. Out in the harbour, a French munitions ship, the *Mont-Blanc*, collided with a Norwegian ship, the *Imo*. *Mont-Blanc* caught fire. She was stuffed to the gills with explosives.

Understandably, her crew promptly abandoned ship. She drifted towards the pier and ran aground. Coleman was warned about her cargo by fleeing sailors. The problem – well, there are many problems in this scenario, aren't there? But the main one – was that the overnight express train was about to pass by. The train had hundreds of passengers aboard. There were more trains behind it.

Coleman sat in his office, repeatedly sending the following in Morse code: 'Hold up the train.' Ammunition ship afire in harbour making for Pier 6 and will explode. Guess this will be my last message. Good-bye, boys.

The train was stopped. The passengers were saved when the ship went up – an enormous explosion, hurling heavy equipment up to 6 miles away. Coleman went up with it, just as he knew he would.

No more needs to be said.

CHAPTER 79

AFTER ALL, HE'S JUST A MAN

Henrietta Maria was the wife of Charles I (and daughter of Henry IV of France; Maryland in the USA is named after her). Their marriage was remarkably strong, despite an inauspicious start – Charles sent a stand-in to represent him at the wedding...* Tammy Wynette was almost certainly, alas, not thinking of Henrietta when she exhorted audiences to 'stand by your man' – but my goodness, Henrietta did. As Charles went through his well-known travails with Parliament, Henrietta demonstrated remarkable strength and determination – and chutzpah. Here is just one example of what I mean.

When things moved from dispute to war in the UK, Henrietta took herself off to the Continent and returned with supplies and weapons for the royalist war effort. Sailing from The Hague, she landed at Bridlington and, as royalty did from time to time, promptly imposed herself on a prominent family for food and lodgings.

As it happens, the Stricklands of Boynton Hall were parliamentarians. Indeed, Sir William was a member of Parliament. But he was in London, and Henrietta (and

---

* In his defence, a 'proxy marriage' wasn't that unusual in the 1600s. She was fifteen at the time of the wedding – also not that unusual then. They were married before his coronation, in which, as a Catholic, she was not permitted to play a part. She remained his 'Queen Consort', never crowned herself.

her rather strong entourage...) was hosted, however reluctantly, by Lady Strickland. At the end of dinner, and of course I paraphrase slightly, Henrietta said... Well, that was lovely, thanks for having me, and this is all a bit awkward but you know, things are a bit tight what with the war and everything. I see all this nice silver you've got about the house – I'm afraid my men and I will have to take it all with us when we go. It's just a loan until we win the war, of course... In the meantime, as a token of my gratitude and esteem for your, er, kindness in giving me all this, I shall give you the gift of a nice portrait. It's of... *me*!

How lovely, Lady Strickland no doubt replied through gritted teeth in the face of *force majeure*, as the family silver was whisked from the rooms around her.

Of course, despite Henrietta's tireless efforts, the war was lost, the King executed, the 'loan' never repaid... but at least the portrait remained at Boynton Hall until the 1970s, when the Strickland family flogged it for a packet at auction. Whether it was worth more than the silver in the end remains unknown.

Lesson: in the long term, it's possible that you may gain from what seemed a rum deal at the time. So, take the long view – especially if you can't do anything else.

And PS – standing by your man was a thing amongst strong women before both kinds of music, country *and* western.

CHAPTER 80

KNIGHT OF THE SHIRES

Some of these stories are of great achievements. Some might outrageously be accused of being excuses to stitch together anecdotes about someone. This is one of the latter.

This is the story of Sir Walter Bromley-Davenport, one of the great Knights of the Shires, and one whose obituary kindly euphemised him as having 'a somewhat *simpliste* view of politics'.

Sir Walter was the welterweight boxing champion of the British Army, commissioned into the Grenadier Guards. He raised and commanded a regiment from his beloved Cheshire upon the outbreak of the Second World War. It is possible that this background influenced his approach to politics.

MP for Knutsford for twenty-five years, he was renowned for bellowing for quiet in meetings of his fellow members, upbraiding the ill-discipline evidenced in the modern era by 'you young officers'. He would invariably scream at Labour MPs to take their hands out of their pockets. Whilst his contributions in Parliament generally fell into the category of behaviour later described by a Speaker as 'chuntering from a sedentary position', he did venture once into a junior position in government. It did not end well.

He had been made a whip. On the one hand, one sees the logic. Given his exceptionally loud voice, his passion for discipline and his distinct lack of shyness in administering it, it sort of made sense. On the other hand…

He at least cannot be accused of failing to take his responsibilities seriously. His particular concern, predictably, was lack of discipline. This came to a head when a 10 p.m. vote was scheduled (this was, of course, before the supposedly more family-friendly sitting hours of the modern era). The issue being voted upon doesn't matter. The point is that, as happens to whips from time to time, Bromley-Davenport was having trouble corralling those for whom he was responsible in order to ensure they supported the government. Some whips believe that one catches more flies with honey. Sir Walter did not.

Already perturbed by the frustrating fact that his charges weren't immediately falling into obedient line, in the distance Sir Walter espied one of 'his' MPs sneaking out of the Commons before the vote. His temper rose. He shouted the man's name. The retreating MP ignored him completely. Why, you little…!

Sir Walter ran after the MP and delivered an almighty Bromley-Davenport boot to the miscreant's backside. Only after the MP fell down the stairs as a result did it turn out that it wasn't his MP at all. It was the Belgian ambassador.

Thus ended Sir Walter's career in government. All for just kicking a diplomat down the stairs, he no doubt would have said.

In later life, whilst beloved by most of his constituents, as such people are invariably said to have been, one broke into his home with an axe and sought to do him harm. Sir Walter swiftly saw him off the premises with the battle cry, 'Don't let the NHS get me!'

They don't make them like they used to.

CHAPTER 81

TWINSET, PEARLS, WORLD RECORDS

This is the story of Milly Bruce, all of 5ft tall, who held seventeen world records on land, in the air and on sea.

Milly's love of fast vehicles manifested itself early. She was arrested whilst speeding on her brother's motorcycle, with her collie dog in the sidecar, and was ordered by the court not to drive a motor vehicle again… until she was sixteen. She was once – and this is not to be admired, of course; I merely state it – prosecuted for different speeding offences three days running in the same court, which must have been an odd experience for the Bench.

In 1927, some 270 miles north of the Arctic Circle, the furthest north anyone had ever driven at that point, Milly Bruce and her husband, Victor, planted the Union Jack – in the course of a 6,000-mile tour of Sweden and Finland in a normal saloon car – when they 'ran out of road'.

This was just one of her feats. In the course of her 24-hour continuous driving world record on the track at Montlhéry, she blamed her failure to maintain a higher speed average than a mere 90mph on having taken a swig from her water bottle, which had accidentally been filled with petrol.

The 1927 Monte Carlo Rally saw her successfully complete the course as part of a team which drove 1,700 miles in a famously hard year through fog and ice. She got frostbite. A couple of years later, she'd barely started in the same event when she turned her car over and crashed down a precipice. She was fine. She hitchhiked 20 miles back to the start, had her car recovered and refitted, and still finished first.

She held the Dover–Calais crossing (and back) record by speedboat. She flew solo to Tokyo and back. She broke the world record for the longest distance covered over sea in twenty-four hours (694 nautical miles). She flew in a flying circus. She started her own airline.

Then conflict came to Europe. She undertook night-flying so the army could use her for spotlight target practice before the Second World War and flew an air-ferry service for our forces in France when the war actually got underway.

She drove on the track into her seventies (clocking over 110mph test-driving a Ford at Thruxton) and flew stunts into her eighties. By the time of her death, aged ninety-four, the *Telegraph* had had her obituary on the stocks for sixty years.

This was all done in a time when women weren't supposed to do such things. She ebulliently did them anyway. Feminists sought to claim her as an icon; she politely declined.

Lesson: you be you.

CHAPTER 82

ONE. LAST. TIME.

This is the *Boys' Own*, Roy of the Rovers, sporting ace Down Under story of Alfie Langer and the State of Origin.

The Australians are, pound for pound, the best sporting nation in the world. If you didn't know that, just ask them and they'll tell you. This means that, much as a Spartan might have thought the most formidable opponent it was possible to face in battle was another Spartan, some of the most significant Strayan sporting contests are not international but those that take place within Australia.

In no sport is this more apparent than Rugby League – a hard game, a fast game, a game missing two players from the scrum – and in no competition within the league is this more apparent than the State of Origin series. For a start, it's so exclusive that four of the six Australian states aren't involved. Three matches a year are played to decide the winner: Queensland Maroons or New South Wales Blues. You play for the state that's home to the professional team you first played for. Hence, State of Origin. As that background suggests, this is one of the fiercest rivalries in sport.

For much of the 1980s and 1990s, a standout player for Queensland was Alfie Langer, perhaps the best halfback of his generation and captain of the best team in the league, the Brisbane Broncos.* He hit hard. He ran straight. He inspired others. Who can wish for more from an athlete? In the closing years of the twentieth century, he was an icon for club and state.

But after a hard decade and a half of hard knocks, Alfie decided that enough was enough. He took up a lucrative form of semi-retirement which might to others have the appearance of hard work but to him and the other Australian Spartans was a relaxing pastime... That is to say that Alfie Langer switched to playing professional Rugby League in the United Kingdom.

As he graced the field as captain for the Warrington Wolves, much was said in the ever-calm Australian press about his going. He would be missed, said some. He's too old, said others; we don't need him in the Queensland side any more. Tempers rose. The Prime Minister issued a statement.

Rugby is a team sport. Success and failure are never about only one man. But it is true to say that, without Alfie, Queensland struggled mightily in the 2001 State of Origin. The series was tied 1–1. The final game loomed.

New South Wales loudly mocked the very notion. But

---

* It is possible that I am biased, as I lived near the ground for some time. Broncos matches were the most partisan sporting events I've experienced. If the opposition were on the attack, an announcement about food and beverage offers might be made, or music might be played. If the Broncos were in possession and nearing the opposition's try line, an *unbelievably* loud 'LET'S GO BRONCOS' would be screamed on the public announcement system, and the crowd would go bananas. If the Broncos scored, a gate at one end of the ground would open and a striking woman on a white horse would gallop around the stadium carrying an enormous Broncos flag. It was not an understated affair.

pride was swallowed. In great secrecy, Queensland made the call. We need you, Alfie. Fly around the world, Alfie. Come back and play for us. One. Last. Time. Ken Oath, Alfie cried, and under a false name booked himself on the next Qantas flight out of London.

No secret this big can stay a secret for very long. Soon, his return (the first ever selection in the series of a player in the UK) was known. The night of the game, Australia stood still. Would this man return to triumph or disaster? Twenty-five other players took to the pitch in Brisvegas, but the focus was all on one man. Alfie. Alfie.

Sometimes, fairy tales come true.

The Queensland side – men who had been boys raised in the shadow of Alfie's greatness – were inspired. The Maroons destroyed New South Wales that night. He set up two tries. He scored one himself. Queensland won 40–14.

Sydney's *Daily Telegraph* said it all with a huge banner headline the next morning: 'BLOODY ALF'.

The biggest lesson must be taken not from the game but from the moment of the surprise call. For the fear of failure – of ending a remarkable career on the highest profile of low notes – must have been huge. His biggest opponent, thought about in this way, was his own reputation.

But none of that mattered. When duty called, Alfie served.

CHAPTER 83

HOW VERY DARE YOU

This is a story about Thomas Moore. No, not Sir Thomas More. Thomas Moore.

An Irish poet, Moore is today perhaps best remembered for being blamed for the destruction of his friend Lord Byron's memoirs. But he was a writer and character of some note in his own right.[*]

On one occasion, he was on the receiving end of a remarkably bad review by a chap called Francis Jeffrey in the *Edinburgh Review*. Jeffrey really went to town on him. Moore shouted the odds about what a bounder Jeffrey was, and how if only he wasn't in Edinburgh, which is ever so far away, why, then he'd definitely call him out for a duel. Funny you should say it, his friends replied – amazing luck! He's here in London today! Oh… well, obviously that's great news, said our Thomas.

So, the challenge was issued – 'You are a liar; yes, sir, a liar…' – it seems that at the turn of the nineteenth century, people had a certain style even when phrasing their 'What are you looking at?' vituperative missives to one another.

---

[*] I am told by an Irishman that he's best recalled in Dublin for a Joycean joke: Moore's statue in Dublin is right by a pissoir, and Joyce has Leopold Bloom reflect upon (a Moore poem) 'The Meeting of the Waters' as he passes it.

Chalk Farm was named as the site of the duel. What the good burghers of that blameless borough would make of it if they knew their suburban bliss was the venue of such a thing is unknown to me.

It was quite a to-do. A surgeon had been arranged to deal with the awful possibilities of mortal combat. Many friends of those on both sides and other spectators besides took themselves to witness the duel, despite the early hour and even though it was in Zone 2.

The distance was solemnly measured. The parties processed in hushed silence to their appointed places. Much fuss was made of the guns being prepared by seconds and pressed into the hands of those fated to this awful moment. A dramatic moment of calm. The signal to fire was about to be given…

Then, *would you believe it*, the peelers arrived in great number. It's almost as if this literary feud had been telegraphed about the land in a way that even the most ignorant policeman couldn't miss. Cynics might even suggest that someone, heaven forbid, had directly tipped them off! The pistols were seized by the police and the ferocious participants were hauled off to Bow Street station, no doubt ever so frustrated by their inability to get at it.

Whilst incarcerated there together awaiting charge – and how conversation goes from 'I want to kill you' to 'I wonder what you thought about the last edition of…' remains unknown to history – the chaps got to chatting about literature and realised that they got on rather well.

Thus began the unlikely lifelong friendship between Thomas Moore and Francis Jeffrey.[*]

One postscript. Rumours – outrageous rumours! – that the guns[†] weren't loaded haunted Moore for the rest of his life. Why, even Byron was thought to have said it. Moore was naturally just furious and said he'd have to call out Byron, if only he weren't overseas at the time, oh, it's just so unfortunate…

---

[*] Whilst friendships were a comfort to him no doubt, Moore went on to have a sad life. His wife and all five of his children predeceased him.

[†] Or even worse, only that of his opponent.

CHAPTER 84

THE FLYING SIKH

This is the story of Hardit Singh Malik, 'The Flying Sikh'.

Malik was born in the Punjab towards the end of the nineteenth century, into a wealthy family. His passion for flight developed early, and he competed against others in flying kites with cords coated in powdered glass, which one used to cut up one's rival's kites. Don't say you didn't learn something today.

He was schooled in the UK and went up to Balliol College, Oxford, not long before the First World War. Blues in cricket and golf followed, and he was playing for Sussex against Kent on the day war with Germany was declared. He tried to join up – but was told he was the wrong colour. So, he volunteered for the French Red Cross, spending over a year driving an ambulance on the Western Front. Through this he applied to and was accepted by the fledgling French Air Service. His Oxford tutor asked our own Royal Flying Corps (RFC) why his brave pupil wasn't good enough for the British forces if our French allies would have him, and via this handy connection he was commissioned by the RFC in 1917.

Thus, he apparently became the first Indian in any flying service in the world. He stood out amongst his peers as the sole fighter pilot sporting a turban and beard, later wearing an oversized helmet to fit over his turban – hence the affectionate nickname 'The Flying Hobgoblin'.

He got his wings in less than a month and was soon qualified to fly the Sopwith Camel. So it was that by repeated insistence of his desire to serve that this man found himself in some of the biggest dogfights in the history of aviation, in the most intense period of combat in the air in the last two years of the First World War.

In one such battle, as over a hundred British and German fighters scrapped above the trenches, Singh shot down his first German. Modern sensibilities might not care for the way he recollected it: 'After much manoeuvring, each trying to get on the other's tail, I got him and had the satisfaction of seeing him go down in flames.'

One attack, in October 1917, saw Malik's unit in pursuit of the Red Baron's Flying Circus, which younger readers will be surprised to know was actually a thing and not just a Monty Python gag. They were caught by surprise by a large number of German fighters. Whilst Malik shot one down, his aircraft was struck by over 400 bullets, two of which pierced his leg. The bullets that hit him had come through the fuel tank, slowing their velocity if rather increasing the risk of fire. Injured and unable to climb with his petrol tank holed, Malik still shot the German down. Seriously wounded and with his petrol tank hit, he crash-landed in Flanders. He survived, having lost much blood and broken his nose.

After a stint in hospital, he rejoined his squadron in

Italy. Where the Germans failed, biology succeeded: he developed an allergy to the castor oil used in the Sopwith Camel's rotary engine and was sent home.

Towards the end of the war, Malik returned to service flying home-defence missions from Biggin Hill. During this posting, he had a break in the London home of a wealthy family which had been converted into a hospital for the RAF, when his nose was finally operated on. He recalled living in real luxury, including drinking wine from the family's well-equipped cellars, which were at the patients' disposal. My sort of hospital.

After his operation, he was redeployed to France and was there until the Armistice. After the war, he returned home. He thought about joining the Indian RAF, but the forces in peacetime was less open-minded than during war, and he again ran into a colour bar. So, he joined the Indian civil service, became Prime Minister of Patiala State – a position which saw him becoming quietly influential in India's progress to independence. He also served as Indian high commissioner to Canada and then ambassador to France and was instrumental as a politician in committee work that saw Indian officer cadets finally trained in a programme that led to the founding of the Indian Air Force in 1932.

After retirement in 1957, he returned to his first love, golf, becoming one of India's finest players – despite two German bullets still embedded in his leg.

'The Flying Hobgoblin' died on 31 October 1985, three weeks before his ninety-first birthday.

CHAPTER 85

THE IRISH CROWN JEWELS

The Irish Crown Jewels were not crown jewels; they were the jewels of the Order of St Patrick, the equivalent of the English Order of the Garter and the Scottish Order of the Thistle. They contained 394 jewels from the collection of English Crown Jewels, gifted in 1831. They were worn by the order's grand master – the lord lieutenant of Ireland, the viceroy of Ireland, the grand poobah of Ireland, the living symbol of British power in Ireland – a status that obviously made him hugely popular with all Irishmen.

In 1907, the lord lieutenant was the Earl of Aberdeen, and the jewels were kept in the Bedford Tower at Dublin Castle, in the safekeeping – or not – of the Ulster King of Arms, Sir Arthur Vicars.

The castle, as may be thought obvious, was something of a focal point for discontent and was guarded around the clock by both the police and the army. There was a strongroom, but – snafu – after building it, the A-team guarding the place found that the safe was too big to go through the door. So, the jewels were kept in the safe in the library. Sir Arthur had the keys for it – one at home; one on him at all times.

Alas, Sir Arthur was both forgetful and a boozer of impressive pedigree. Famously, after one suitably heavy session, he woke up wearing the jewels, as he'd passed out and his chums had unlocked the safe and dressed him in them.

So... security wasn't great.

One fine Dublin summer morning, the Bedford Tower cleaning lady found the first door of the strongroom left open. The inner door was still locked – but the ring of keys which opened both the strongroom and the library were there in the lock.

Sir Arthur was not one to panic. Indeed, his blasé implacability might be discerned from the fact that he didn't bother to check the safe after the open doors were discovered. It was only later that day, when sending someone to put something in it, that it was discovered – and this will be a great surprise to you – that the jewels were gone. As ill luck would have it, Edward VII was due in town for the investment of a new member of the order that week. His Majesty was... not impressed. The ceremony (alas, poor blameless newbie) was cancelled.

The Dublin Metropolitan Police investigated. I think that we can agree to a certain amount of pity for the chap who was passed this case.

Suspect #1 – stand by for another shock – was Sir Arthur Vicars. Means, yes. Opportunity, yes. Motive... well, money, perhaps? The jewels were worth a packet. But Vicars had no financial problems, and he was hardly likely to fence the jewels successfully – so on motive, nothing really. Besides, whilst there was ample evidence of magnificent levels of incompetence, there wasn't any actual evidence against him. But he was still fired. Sir Arthur protested his innocence until the day he died, which was quite soon as – unsportingly, given how amply he'd demonstrated the fallibility of British aristocratic office-holders – the IRA killed him.

Suspect #2 – Pierce O'Mahony, Sir Arthur's assistant (and half-brother). No evidence against him, beyond the obvious association with a dim-witted boss.

Suspect #3 – Francis Shackleton, explorer Ernest Shackleton's brother and Sir Arthur's second-in-command at the castle. Maybe he did it, but he was never charged. Quite separately, he was convicted of fraud in 1914, so he was plainly a wrong 'un, which might be thought indicative. Shackleton changed his name and vanished, never to be seen again, after finishing his sentence. Again, you might very well think and so on and so forth. Means and opportunity (lifting keys from a regular toper of a boss) – yes. Motive… obviously he was keen on cash, and willing to go to ground…

Suspect #4 – Francis Bennett-Goldney. He was totally unsuspected at the time and rejoicing in the title athlone pursuivant, which was Dublin Castle's equivalent of vice-president at a US bank – i.e. very junior. Like others, he had means and opportunity, but nobody saw a motive – until he died in a car crash in 1918 and a load of stolen goods were found stashed at his house. But no crown jewels were amongst the booty, and there was no evidence to connect him to them either.

That's the whole list of suspects. You will note that

despite all the tension in these islands over Home Rule at the time, it lacks any hint of republicanism, or of an attack on the government of the day and so forth. This, it seems, was simply about venality and incompetence and was an all-British affair.

The investigation – for want of leads or for fear of what else it might uncover amongst the louche Brits boozing away their days at the castle – petered out. The jewels remain missing to this day.* So does F. Shackleton.† The order's last knight died, jewel-less, in 1974.

Lesson: if you are charged with the grave and weighty responsibility of selecting a man to guard priceless jewels, offer him a brandy. Then offer him another. Then offer him another and so on. If he's on the deck before the end of the interview, perhaps re-open nominations.

---

* There is an intriguing memorandum in the papers of the new Irish State, which came to light on the public record some fifty years after it was written in 1927. It seems that an offer to sell the jewels to the new country had been made, by person or persons unknown. Whether the offer was genuine or not remains a mystery, and the offer was not pursued.

† For what it's worth: i) Sir Arthur publicly accused Shackleton of being responsible. His views counted for very little; ii) the Scotland Yard detective sent to assist the investigation countered these allegations by publicly asserting that Shackleton *wasn't* involved – but given the rather limited success of the investigation, his account is not to be regarded as canonical either.

CHAPTER 86

CREATIVE DIFFERENCES

Whilst apparently endlessly entertaining for some, spats between celebrities are not uncommon. And though there are exceptions, they tend not to lead to multiple deaths.

Edwin Forrest was a homegrown stage-star at a time when the arts in America were establishing a life independent of the former colonial ruler; William Charles Macready was a famous English actor. They were friends, but they fell out as they disagreed about who was the better Shakespearean leading man. So far, so Tupac / Biggie Smalls.

Their dispute became a *cause célèbre*, not least because it served as a focal point in the wider, rather poor 1840s US–UK relationship. Thus who was the better, say, Othello stood as a proxy for Yanks and their allies bashing the Brits, and for the Brits and their allies bashing the Yanks.

Plainly things have changed a bit since, but of the two sides it was the US press that was especially vituperative at the time. There was also something of a class-struggle-within-American-society element to the dispute, with Man of the People Forrest against All You Snooty Toffs Prefer Him Macready. Suitably for a champion of a young and vigorous culture, Forrest was a muscular and ebullient man; suitably for the derided representative of an old world that had had its day, Macready was more subtle and gentle – or effete, as his critics would have put it.

Macready repeatedly toured the USA; Forrest repeatedly toured the UK. We are better at this than you are, each tour seemed to declare. At the beginning, one might charitably say that that was just how it seemed to those who wished to see it that way. At the end, it was what the players were saying themselves.

During Macready's second American tour, Forrest followed him around the country and put on the same plays in the same towns in the same weeks. Forrest's final UK tour bombed, and he blamed Macready. So, he turned up to Macready's *Hamlet* and loudly booed him. Macready declared – and these are plainly fighting words – that Forrest was 'without taste'. Handbags, really. I mean, thus far these chaps are boxers trash-talking one another at the pre-fight publicity event, but without the possibility of an actual, er, fight.

Or so they would have thought.

On Macready's third (and final) American tour, half a dead sheep was thrown upon the stage. What happened to the other half remains unknown. This is the sort of thing that can put a chap right off his soliloquy.

Things came to a head in May 1849…

Macready was doing *Macbeth* at the Astor Place Opera House, later the Astor Place Theater (note my immaculate American spelling, which hurt to type) and either way alas no longer with us, which stood by the junction of Broadway and the Bowery in New York. Forrest, would you credit it, was doing *Macbeth* the same night at the Broadway Theater nearby.

The Astor Place Theater / Theatre, which henceforth I will just call the Astor, had grand ambitions. It was a bastion of the establishment and had a dress code designed to put off most people. In the febrile atmosphere of the day, it might as well have painted a target upon itself.

On 7 May 1849, Forrest's champions bought hundreds of tickets in the Gods of the Astor and pelted Macready with rotten eggs. When that didn't do it, shoes and seats ripped up from their rows followed. The performance was stopped.

That same night, when Forrest as Macbeth in his rival production gave the Nicola Sturgeon line, 'What rhubarb, senna or what purgative drug will scour these English hence?' the audience rose to its feet and cheered.

Plainly it was all going to kick off.

Macready, who whatever his faults cannot be said to have lacked guts, took to the stage for his next performance as scheduled on 10 May. No doubt he said to himself, 'The show must go on' and so forth. Admirable but, in hindsight, perhaps foolhardy.

(An interposition. Theatre riots weren't that uncommon at the time. The theatre – with no disrespect to the stage today – was perhaps the foremost form of mass entertainment in that age, and from time to time audiences

expressed their views, shared or divergent, on both performance and politics in vigorous ways.)

Thus it was that the militia was called out before the
performance even started: the police and mayoralty of
NYC realised that they didn't have the policing manpower
to stop what was brewing. What does the militia look like
in New York City in the 1840s? Well, it's the New York
State 7th regiment, plus cavalry, hussars and artillery. You
say overkill; they say can't be too careful. This, a force of
350, plus 250 policemen will do it and ensure peace, the
mayor no doubt said to himself.

But, as we reflected in the story of the Day of the Tiles
back in Chapter 20, generally speaking there are good reasons not to put troops on the streets at times of concern
about law and order. First, there is a distinction between
a civilian society policing itself and the army imposing
law on it; between civil and martial law. Second, once you
press the 'go' button, once the army is deployed, it does
what it does. Armies are for fighting.

Anyway. That day, all over the city, handbills were given
out calling on people to come to express their views about
the British in no uncertain terms. Macready's show was a
sell-out, but alas not for the reasons he might have hoped.
Macbeth opened at the Astor on time at 7.30 p.m., and
that's the last thing that went as planned.

A crowd of 10,000 had gathered around the Astor.
They bombarded it with stones, passed helpfully to the
front as with so many peaceful demonstrations today, and

fought in the street with the police. Simultaneously, their allies inside tried (and failed) to set the building on fire. Macready finished the play, pantomiming as – you'll be shocked – he couldn't be heard above the din, and escaped the building.

The army was called in. You'll never guess what happened next.

The soldiers were not received with open arms by the demonstrators. They were mocked, pushed, pelted and hurt. Then the army did what the army does. A line was formed. Warnings, which no doubt couldn't be heard above the din anyway, were given and not heeded. They opened fire.

As usual, order was restored. As usual, the cost was high.

Repeated point-blank volleys into a crowd have an obvious result. Definitive numbers are unclear but something between twenty to thirty rioters (and bystanders) died, and over 120 people were injured. Seventy policemen and over 140 militiamen were injured.

For the arts, it's claimed that this dispute led to a bifurcation in the theatre between the world of the working man and that of the upper class, with Shakespeare alas falling from popularity as a form of mass entertainment. Perhaps a claim too far, but what a cost.

For the authorities, aversion to relying on the militia in such circumstances led to significantly increased firepower for the American police – an escalation one might say can be seen to this day.

Lesson: perhaps, when someone says he does a better Coriolanus than you, you might simply reply, 'You're just jealous.' Or, you know, blank him. You never know where the argument might go.

CHAPTER 87

WHEN LEPIDORAE ATTACK

Napoleon won the War of the Fourth Coalition, but he lost the celebration after. Lest this seem obscure, I remind you of the most dangerous enemy faced by Monty Python's King Arthur: the Legendary Black Beast of Arrrghhh, against which, after heavy losses, the Holy Hand Grenade of Antioch had to be deployed.

It was like this: the treaty had been signed. Success was affirmed. Napoleon's chief of staff, Louis-Alexandre Berthier, was confronted with the typical gift challenge: what to get the Emperor who has everything?

Well, he thought, Napoleon does like to hunt.

So, Berthier invited the army's top brass and bought a ton of target victims for the occasion. What could be more sociable and less risky than armed men blasting thousands of rabbits to smithereens over drinks?

Except it didn't work out like that.

The guns were handed out. The brandies were passed around. Cigars were lit. The cages were unlocked. But the rabbits, rather than running away from Napoleon, ran... towards him. Ha ha, those present must have laughed... the laughter drying up in speechless mouths as the rabbits kept on coming, an enormous swarm soon surrounding them and then climbing... up them.

For it turned out that these rabbits were not wild but domesticated, expected the bipeds present to feed them and had no fear of them. Never previously released in one place in such numbers, they were swiftly utterly uncontrollable, and all men present were soon, well, covered in rabbits.

Attendants tried to beat them with staffs, but it's hard to do that without whacking the man underneath. The rabbits kept coming. They seemed endless.

'RUN AWAY!' cried Napoleon – in my imagination at least. Napoleon's fastest retreat ended in him unceremoniously legging it for his carriage. Even there, many rabbits had made it into the carriage either before or whilst he was boarding, and had to be combated as the Emperor sped away from the shortest, worst party in the history of the First French Empire.

CHAPTER 88

BROKE OF THE SHANNON

This is the story of a great son of Suffolk, Philip Broke, and of his ship, the *Shannon*.

In 1812, Britain was at war with the United States. Contrary to expectations, the Americans were thumping the Royal Navy at every turn. Bigger ships, heavier guns, larger crews.

Broke was to change things.

The crew of the *Shannon* drilled tirelessly. Their captain set them challenge after challenge. Gunnery practice. Swordplay. Scenarios: imagine we are being attacked in such and such a way – what do we do? Fire the guns blindfolded, with instructions on your target given orally. It was this dedicated crew and their ship that blockaded Boston. A fierce hunger to do that which their comrades had not – to take on and beat one of these great Yank ships – burnt within them. In the harbour lay one such: James Lawrence's ship, the USS *Chesapeake*. Come out, come out, the *Shannon* cried. We are ready whenever you are.

In the meantime, ship after ship was seized as it sought to enter or leave Boston harbour. Broke sent them off as prizes to British North America. But soon, this threatened to leave him undermanned for any real fight, as he had to man each such ship with a prize crew drawn from his own. So, he did something extraordinary. He burnt his prizes. In a navy in which men made fortunes from what they captured, it is a mark of the fervour of this captain – and the loyalty of his crew – that this was done. The little boats belonging to the burnt ships were sent into Boston with their crews aboard, and those men took with them the message – again and again – from the *Shannon*: come and fight, *Chesapeake*.

Broke feared that Lawrence might never put to sea to fight. Ultimately, he wrote to him – as Lawrence had earlier written to a British captain. He (accurately) described his ship, pointing out that they were relatively evenly matched. And then he went in for some nineteenth-century burns:

> I entreat you, sir, not to imagine that I am urged by mere personal vanity to the wish of meeting the Chesapeake, or that I depend only upon your personal ambition for your acceding to this invitation. We have both noble motives.
>
> You will feel it as a compliment if I say that the result of our meeting may be the most grateful service I can render to my country; and I doubt not that you, equally confident of success, will feel convinced that it is only by repeated triumphs in even combats that your little navy can now hope to console your country for the loss of that trade it can no longer protect. Favour me with a speedy reply. We are short of provisions and water, and cannot stay long here.

Challenge made. Challenge accepted.*

With an earlier command, Lawrence had given a poorly performing British ship a thrashing, and he almost certainly underestimated his opponent as a result. A berth in Boston's dock was reserved for the ship he was to capture. A victory party was planned.

With every vantage point and height along the shore crammed with spectators, the *Chesapeake* put to sea, with some of Boston's keenest warwatchers following her in boats to get the best view of the inevitable triumph that was to take place.

The ships were almost exactly the same length and width. The guns were even enough as to make no difference. The *Chesapeake* was a little heavier. She had a crew of 379 whilst the *Shannon* had 330. It was to be a fairly matched fight.

They met 20 miles off the coast, between Cape Cod and Cape Ann. Both ships held their fire until at close range. Many of the American shots went into the water, but their carronade fire went into an ammunition store, sending shot through the British ship viciously.

Still, the *Shannon* had the better of it. Her crew fired into the decks to kill, rather than aiming to dismast for a well-kept prize. Broke's crew knew what they were doing, moment to moment, for their captain had drilled them until each step came naturally – even if they couldn't see in the fog of war. Historian Josephus said of the legions

---

* Lawrence probably didn't get the letter, but that rather spoils the story.

of Rome that their drills were bloodless battles and their battles were bloody drills. Thus fought Broke and his men of the *Shannon*.

The *Chesapeake*'s wheel was shot away. Some sail was lost. She yawed. The ships drew closer and the *Shannon*'s crew lashed them together, though one lost an arm in the doing of it. British fire remorselessly diminished the *Chesapeake*'s crew. When the time was right, they boarded her.

Lawrence was mortally wounded. His lieutenant, William Cox, who had served with him all his sailing life, carried him below deck. His last words were, 'Tell the men to fire faster. Don't give up the ship!'

Sharpshooters in the rigging blasted away at each other. Some American guns still fired. Fighting on the deck was fierce. Americans rallied and counter-attacked. But the outcome was increasingly brutally clear. Broke led the charge against the last knot of American resistance. As he did so, the ships were blown apart, leaving the boarding party stranded. Americans coming down the rigging surprised Broke and wounded him, a sabre cut to the head sending him to the deck.

The crew of the *Shannon* rallied to their captain. They charged and surrounded the fallen Broke. Most of the Americans were killed. The remaining Americans below deck (with some suggestions of cowardice in seeking refuge there lamented by one of their officers) surrendered.

In a little over ten minutes, more than 200 men had been killed or injured. Twenty-three of the *Shannon*'s men were killed, and fifty-six were wounded. *Chesapeake* had forty-eight killed and ninety-nine wounded. It was one of the bloodiest single ship actions of the age.

The *Shannon*, with a lieutenant commanding her whilst Broke recovered from his wound, escorted the *Chesapeake* to Halifax as a prize. She became HMS *Chesapeake* of the Royal Navy. Broke was made a baronet. Lawrence was buried with honours at Halifax, with British officers his pallbearers. History now records that Lawrence rushed into the fight with an underprepared crew, overconfident of victory and (for understandable reasons) underestimating an opponent who was far better prepared than he expected. After all, both sides took great punishment, but only one broke. But still: we can recognise the bravery shown on both sides – especially by the captains, who led their men from the front to great personal cost.

Broke was never to command a ship again. His wound was grievous. The sabre had penetrated his head by at least three inches. He lived semi-crippled to the age of sixty-four.

The lessons here will sound like they're from a sports or management manual, but they are unavoidable: practise until action is second nature. Never underestimate your opponent. Remorseless focus tends to win, even when held by an outnumbered, unfancied contender. Broke showed all this.

CHAPTER 89

FLYING DOWN THE AVENUE

Baron Jean de Selys Longchamps was a grand-nephew of King Leopold III of Belgium, who had a bad war (the King was resented for surrendering his country to Hitler, no matter how inevitable such surrender might have been, and he was forced later to abdicate in favour of his son in the face of great public resentment).

De Selys, who was in the Belgian cavalry when the Second World War was declared, was made of sterner stuff. He saw action in the forlorn, eighteen-day Battle of Belgium,* and after the Belgian surrender in May 1940 he sought to rally Belgian forces against the Nazis from France – efforts that inevitably failed, given the Franco-German armistice.

He tried to get to the UK via Morocco to continue in the war effort but was held as a prisoner of war in Marseille before escaping and getting to Britain via Spain. Once in the UK, he joined the Royal Air Force, in which he served bravely. But he lived with one overriding, burning passion: to avenge the death of his father, who had been killed by the Gestapo in Brussels. Understandably

---

* The German official history of the war noted the 'extraordinary bravery' of the Belgian Armed Forces in this conflict, which included the Battle of Hannut, the largest tank battle in history at the time – so you must not think that a cavalryman had things easy.

denied permission by the RAF to carry out a lone fighter plane attack, he did what Captain Kirk did when refused permission to use the Starship *Enterprise* to rescue Spock – he did it anyway.

In January 1943, he took part in an attack on a railway junction near Ghent. So far, so in obedience with orders. That mission went to plan. But then, keeping low so as to avoid radar detection, he departed from the mission plan and flew on alone to Brussels, where he buzzed down the famous Avenue Louise. Gestapo headquarters was on said avenue – and was where his father had been tortured to death. He machine-gunned the building, wrecking the facade, killing four Germans and injuring many others. This was some precision flying: the buildings either side of the HQ remained completely untouched.

As he escaped the scene unscathed, he executed the *pièce de résistance*: he opened his cockpit and dropped thousands of miniature Belgian and British flags over Brussels. Half an hour later, he was safely back at base at Manston.

That big building on Avenue Louise had been hated by the *Bruxellois*; now they came to see its wrecked state and took heart. Those listening clandestinely to BBC news reports soon spread the word across the whole country that the deed had been done by one of their own. The boost to Belgian morale was huge.

De Selys was simultaneously demoted to pilot officer for disobedience and awarded the Distinguished Flying Cross for bravery. He died in a crash-landing at Manston soon after, having been hit during a raid over Ostend.

It's impossible not to admire the man. I imagine that those demoting him did. He risked not only his life but also a valuable aircraft in doing as he did. Armed forces can't have pilots jetting off on frolics of their own, no matter how heartfelt and no matter how successful – especially in wartime. But one can tip a knowing wink to the brave after – as we did, giving to de Selys with one hand as we took away with the other.

What's the lesson to take from de Selys and his raid? If disobeying orders, your scheme had better come off. And the more stylish the better, I suppose.

CHAPTER 90

YOUR TURN

On the first day of the Battle of the Somme, the most profligate day in the history of the British Army, Basil Liddell Hart* and his close friend Lancelot Spicer† were junior officers sent to relieve those who'd first gone over the top. (Spicer was later to note that of the twenty-three officers from his battalion who had gone into the line ahead of them that morning, twenty-one were either killed or seriously wounded by the evening.)

It was a rush job to get their relief force into place. Spicer peremptorily took command of their unit. Liddell Hart, who was not shy, resented him doing so. They disputed the issue for some fifty years. On reading Liddell Hart's memoirs in 1965, Spicer wrote to him: 'Now ... I understand your irritation. I just assumed I was senior. Next time,' the 72-year-old wrote to his friend, 'I'll leave it to you.'

---

* Liddell Hart was 'the captain who taught generals' – a military strategist of some renown, and it is fair to say not unfamiliar with a touch of self-promotion.

† In a peculiar coincidence that touches on the sacrifice our country called on families to make generation after generation at that time, Spicer's son served in the same unit as his father in the Second World War.

CHAPTER 91

FANTASIA

It is difficult to imagine this one happening anywhere other than Italy.

During the Cold War, the Terzo Corpo designato d'Armata was Italy's north-eastern force prepared to repel the Russian tanks as they rolled westwards. It comprised some 300,000 men and was based in the Venice area for some decades.

Or not. In fact, rather than going to the trouble of calling up or recruiting and then training and arming men in that kind of volume, the Italians thought it was a lot easier just to lie about it. The Terzo Corpo designato d'Armata never existed apart from a commanding officer with a secretarial staff. Their job was to pump out documentation that would support the fictitious life of such a force. Recruitment papers. Ammunition requisition. Mustering out documentation. Manoeuvres. Paperwork by the ton, deliberately leaked to spies in order to convince the Soviets that Italy would be robustly defended if they invaded Western Europe. A gargantuan and successful bluff from the 1950s until 1972, when the force was 'disbanded'.

How did this fiction come to light? A sleuthing historian in the military archives? An exchange between military veterans, in which an incredulous Russian finally learns from his former counterpart that the unit they'd diligently mapped on order of battle charts, recording the strengths of opposing forces, was a fiction?

No. It emerged in the early twenty-first century, long after the Cold War had ended, because the Italians had tied themselves in a procedural knot that could only happen to Italians and they started complaining about it. Documents certified as 'secret' in Italy can only be destroyed once they are declassified. They can only be declassified by the department or military unit that created them. But in this case, that unit had been disbanded. And had never existed anyway. So – to my knowledge, even to this day – the Italian Army is stuck with over twenty years' worth of truly mountainous warehousefuls of fictitious paperwork, all at least fifty years old, in barracks and archives and offices all over the country, that it cannot destroy.

I read about this in John Hooper's excellent book *The Italians*, in which he describes it as an example of 'fantasia' – 'a word whose meaning lies somewhere on the permeable frontier between "imagination" and "creativity"'. Which is funny, as it applies sublimely to the creation of the corps but is a spirit plainly defeated utterly by Italian bureaucracy.

CHAPTER 92

THE UNKILLABLE ADRIAN

Adrian Carton de Wiart served his country in the Second Boer War, the First World War and the Second World War. In the course of these conflicts, he was shot in the ankle, ear, face, groin, head, hip, leg and stomach. He was blinded in one eye. When a doctor refused to amputate his badly injured fingers on the Western Front, he pulled them off himself. Asked to describe his time in the trenches, he said, 'Frankly, I had enjoyed the war.'

Let's take all that a little more slowly.

From Belgian aristocratic stock, Carton de Wiart boarded in the UK and then went to Oxford,* leaving early to join the British Army under a false name and inflated age. Travelling out to South Africa, he was soon invalided back with serious belly and groin injuries. He recovered, was commissioned into the Imperial Light Horse, sent back out to SA and when conflict finished, he headed with his regiment to India for what was recalled in later times as his 'halcyon years' of polo and pig-sticking.

When the First World War was declared, he was caught somewhat, as he was on his way with the Somaliland

---

* A university of sorts.

Camel Corps* to take part in an altogether smaller conflict between British forces and the supporters of the – woke word warriors look away now, and / or remember that it was the past; they did things differently there – 'Mad Mullah' Mohammed bin Abdullah in Somaliland. Take part he did, getting shot in the arm and in the face (twice) and losing an eye and a chunk of an ear. Injured as he was mid-battle, he had to remain with his unit for some time in agony before his face could be treated.

Let us agree that having been gutshot would have stopped most of us from further conflict, and having been gutshot and shot twice in the face would do it for pretty much all of us. But this chap was just getting started. Soon he was off to France, where in the course of the war he was wounded a total of eight times.† He was shot through the skull (the back of his head – an incredibly lucky injury to have survived) and the ankle at the Somme, the hip at Passchendaele, the leg at Cambrai and the ear at Arras. Having lost his left hand in 1915 (as previously mentioned pulling off the fingers himself, with the amputation of the rest of it done later), his men describe seeing him pulling the pins from grenades with his teeth before lobbing them

---

* Not to be confused with the Imperial Camel Corps. Both were wonderfully eccentric and surprisingly effective military units; it is the Imperial that has a beautiful but absurdly small memorial on Victoria Embankment. The camel atop it is about the size of a squirrel. One wonders if they sent off the measurements missing a zero on each dimension.

† The nursing facility in London to which he returned to recuperate after each injury became so accustomed to his regular visits that they kept his pyjamas for him.

with his remaining hand at the Somme, where he won the Victoria Cross.

This does, you might think, rather tack against the Melchett tendency for which senior army officers in the First World War have been criticised. For his part, Carton de Wiart didn't even mention his VC in his memoirs – for, in his view, it had been won by everyone in his unit rather than just by him, so it was invidious to draw attention to any individual honour.

After the war, he went to join the British military mission in Poland, which he soon led. In keeping with the story about Britain's magnificent Polish allies and the Cichociemni in Chapter 30, he felt very strongly about the importance of helping and defending that country and begged any political figure who would listen – and some who wouldn't – to give Poland more support. The Second World War might have been rather different if he had prevailed.*

Rather less clear-cut was his acting as a second in a duel during this stint in Poland. Plainly this is out of keeping with the mores of our time, and even of his, but wholly in keeping with his own worldview.

One is conscious that a single line in a potted biography of this man would constitute whole books about others. How's this: during his time in Poland, he was in

---

* The only sympathetic ear he found, in a sign of their early and thereafter consistent understanding, was Churchill's. Too late and too little but still better than nothing, Churchill managed to get *some* materiel from Britain to Poland, against Lloyd George's wishes.

a plane crash on the wrong side of a contentious border: he survived (obviously), and it led to a stint as a prisoner of the Lithuanians. Released by them soon enough, their view of this remarkable man remains unrecorded, but I daresay they weren't sorry to be shot of him. Soon after the Russian Revolution, with the Soviets at the gates of Warsaw, our man was on a train attacked by Red cavalry. He fought them off with his pistol, briefly falling from the train before reboarding.

He 'retired' in the 1920s with the honorary rank of major general. Do you think a life of rest and tranquillity followed? Of course you don't. Gifted a huge estate by Polish aristocracy, he enjoyed a period of peace and daily hunting, but the looming Second World War saw him recalled to active duty.

Put back in his old role leading the British military mission to Poland, his counsel to get the Polish fleet out of the Baltic was accepted and ensured it played a useful part in Allied activities in the war. Alas, his advice with regard to strategic retrenchment of Polish land forces, moving them behind the Vistula river, was ignored.

As his mission was evacuated, his convoy was attacked by the Luftwaffe; his aide's wife was killed. He crossed into Romania and escaped on a false passport.

He took command of a scrambled Anglo-French force in Norway. He was in a reconnaissance plane that was shot up by a German fighter, but he (unlike others) was unharmed. The whole campaign was a fiasco

– under-resourced, lacking air or artillery cover, without even the proper skiing equipment. But he was ordered to hold his ground, so he did.

When finally evacuated (by Lord Mountbatten!), Carton de Wiart found himself at Scapa Flow. It was his sixtieth birthday. He was posted to command defences in Northern Ireland, told he was too old and stood down, then reactivated to command in Yugoslavia, where Nazi invasion loomed. (Meanwhile the Soviets had overrun his Polish home, stealing his possessions and laying waste to the estate. He was never to return.)

On his way to Belgrade, the engines on his plane failed and he crash-landed in the sea a mile from the Libyan shore. The shock of the cold water restored the stunned Carton de Wiart to consciousness, and he swam to shore with his crew, where they were captured by the Italians.

Now it was the turn of the Italians to have this irrepressible man as a prisoner. He made five escape attempts, including one that involved digging a tunnel for seven months. One attempt was less unsuccessful than the others, and he spent over a week on the run in Italy in disguise. Without reducing our admiration one jot, let us agree that there is something rather comical about this man, who was of undeniably distinctive appearance being minus an eye and minus a hand, and who spoke not a word of Italian, successfully passing himself off as an Italian peasant for five minutes, let alone over a week.

By the summer of 1943, the Italians were keen to get out of the war and killed two birds with one stone by sending this troublesome prisoner to take part in their negotiations, releasing him back to London.

But not for long. Soon he was off to China as Churchill's representative to negotiate with the nationalist leader Chiang Kai-shek. En route, he attended the famous Cairo conference. He excelled in China (including with the famously prickly American commander Joseph Stilwell, who took to this tough soldier and, I like to think, saw eye to eye with him, if with few others).* He served his country and the Allies well in this important arena and Attlee asked him to stay on in China after the war when Labour took power. Wonderfully, he upbraided the increasingly powerful Mao for not fighting the Japanese sufficiently seriously: from other men this would have been a career-ender, but such was the respect Carton de Wiart commanded that Mao took it with good grace.

Chiang offered him a job in the post-war Chinese set-up, but Carton de Wiart was finally ready to down tools. On his way home, in Rangoon, loose coconut matting did more than many enemy combatants managed: he slipped and fell, breaking several ribs and knocking himself out.

---

* Stilwell's impact on Sino-American relations and the ultimate fate of the anti-communist forces in China is heavily contested by historians: some think him a great general given an impossible task; others blame him for one of the largest single negative political and social developments in history.

But he recovered, came home and, widowed, got remarried to a woman some twenty-three years younger than him.

After the most improbably successful life of combat, Carton de Wiart died peacefully aged eighty-three and is buried in his adopted home in County Cork. A life lived to the full by the unkillable Adrian Carton de Wiart.

CHAPTER 93

LBJ VIGNETTES

Trigger warning – predictably, given that these vignettes are about Lyndon B. Johnson – some of these are profane. And, having grown to the status of legends, may or may not be true – but they are too good to miss.

* * *

Shortly after being sworn in as President on Air Force One after the death of JFK, LBJ and his shellshocked entourage landed at a busy air force base.

A green lieutenant met him at the foot of the stairs and said, 'Over there – that's your helicopter, Mr President.'

LBJ replied, 'Son, they're all my helicopters.'

* * *

To understand the following, it is necessary to understand that from time to time it has been alleged that in certain American elections the names of dead people are gathered and used on falsified ballot papers to bolster support for candidates.

So, LBJ and his team were taking names for the polls from tombstones. It was late. They were tired. A junior aide skipped over a worn headstone that was hard to read.

LBJ stopped him in his tracks: 'Son, that man has got as much of a right to vote as anyone in this graveyard.'

* * *

This one is *especially* profane.

LBJ to his press guy, of an opponent: 'Go out and say he fucks pigs.'

Aide: 'But, sir, he doesn't fuck pigs!'

LBJ: 'Well sure, son. But I want to hear the son of a bitch deny it.'

* * *

Peacock-proud de Gaulle ordered the removal of all American servicemen from French soil. LBJ's response concluded the issue rather quickly: 'Does that include the ones in the cemeteries?'

* * *

One anecdote that's less fruity but still fascinating for politicos and those on the prowl for early signs of the political leader to come: in his biography of the President, Robert Caro says that LBJ brushed his teeth five times in the morning and five times at night whilst at university, so as to casually 'accidentally' meet everyone on his corridor.

* * *

And finally, whilst LBJ said that 'we can draw lessons from the past, but we cannot live in it', he also said: 'Books and ideas are the most effective weapons against intolerance and ignorance.'

CHAPTER 94

A HIGHER AUTHORITY

Once upon a time our leading courts sat in Westminster Hall, the beautiful barn of a building that is the oldest on the parliamentary estate. (That they could once all be accommodated there might be thought instructive.)

The hall's earlier use was shown by the discovery of medieval tennis balls in the rafters, which points to the shared word 'court' between tennis and the law.

Sir Thomas More was a man for all seasons. He became our Lord Chancellor, the highest legal authority in the land under the Crown. But there was another authority he recognised.

On his way to his own court in Westminster Hall, he would pass the court in which his elderly father sat as a (relatively humble) King's Bench judge. The son would stop there to pay his respects; before all who were there, the Lord Chancellor would kneel and ask his father's blessing on the work to be done that day.

Lesson: honour thy father and mother.

ACKNOWLEDGEMENTS

Whilst any mistakes are of course my own, I am grateful to the following kind people, amongst others, for story suggestions: Chris Crampton, Andrew Deane, Jackie Deane, Paul Deane, Polly Dymock, Allan Engel, Gavin Esler, James Fisher, Henry Hill, David Jones, Richard Lilford, Andrew Macallister, Conrad Oliveira de Sousa, David Petrie, Jon Philip, Simon Richards, Lee Rotherham, Alistair Stirling, Catriona Stirling, Elizabeth Stirling, Euan Stirling, Katy Stirling, Seonaid Stirling and Natalie Whiteight; and from Twitter @diventpanicpet, @CaptnCrash, @TraderNeo1 and @CityandLivery.

Those who have been good enough to point out spelling mistakes, neglected details and other errors in the stories posted online are, sadly, too numerous to mention!

James Stephens, Olivia Beattie, Lucy Stewardson, Vicky Jessop and Suzanne Sangster at Biteback have been consistently kind and encouraging as my eccentric tales took their eccentric courses through their highly professional world.

This would not have become a book without the encouragement of the many on Twitter who urged its creation. I am grateful and hope that you think it's come up to scratch. As ever, I'm @ajcdeane to hear what you think – and for more #deanehistory tales!

BIBLIOGRAPHY

Abdullah II of Jordan, *Our Last Best Chance: The Pursuit of Peace in a Time of Peril* (London: Allen Lane, 2011)

Bines, Jeffrey, *The Polish Country Section of the Special Operations Executive 1940–1946: A British Perspective*, PhD thesis, Stirling University, 2008

Boothby, Robert, *Boothby: Recollections of a Rebel* (London: Hutchison, 1976)

Caro, Robert, *The Path to Power: The Years of Lyndon Johnson, Volume 1* (New York: Alfred A. Knopf Inc., 1982)

Danchev, Alex, *Alchemist of War: The Life of Basil Liddell-Hart* (London: Weidenfeld & Nicolson, 1999)

Davis, R. H. C., *A History of Medieval Europe* (London: Longman, Greens & Co., 1957)

Deane, Philip, *Captive in Korea* (London: Hamish Hamilton, 1953)

Esler, Gavin, *The Good Goering*, BBC Radio 4, 27 January 2016, https://www.bbc.co.uk/programmes/b06ycwr4

Farndale, Nigel, *Haw-Haw: The Tragedy of William and Margaret Joyce* (London: Pan Books, 2006)

Glover, Michael, *Wellington's Peninsular Victories* (London: Pan Books, 1971)

Hooper, John, *The Italians* (London: Allen Lane, 2015)

Keene, Raymond, *The World Chess Championship: Korchnoi vs Karpov, The Inside Story of the Match* (London: B. T. Batsford, 1978)

Leasor, James, *The Boarding Party* (London: Heinemann, 1978)

Liddell Hart, Basil H., *The Way to Win Wars* (London: Faber & Faber, 1942)

Macintyre, Ben, *The Spy and the Traitor: The Greatest Espionage Story of the Cold War* (London: Penguin, 2018)

Massingberd, Hugh, *The Daily Telegraph Books of Obituaries: A Celebration of Eccentric Lives* (London: Pan Macmillan, 1995)

Mordal, Jacques, *Twenty-Five Centuries of Sea Warfare* (London: Abbey Library, 1959)

Muggeridge, Malcolm, *Chronicles of Wasted Time, Chronicle 2: The Infernal Grove* (London: Collins, 1973)

Murray, John, *The Great Game: On Secret Service in High Asia* (London: John Murray, 1990)

Murray, Simon, *Legionnaire: Five Years in the French Foreign Legion, the World's Toughest Army* (London: Sidgwick & Jackson, 2001)

Payne Best, Sigismund, *The Venlo Incident* (London: Hutchison, 1950)

Rivlin, Geoffrey, *First Steps in the Law* (Oxford: Oxford University Press, 2002)

Ruler, John, *Cross-Channel France, Nord-Pas de Calais: The Land Beyond the Ports* (London: Bradt Guides, 2010)

Sutherland, James (ed.), *The Oxford Book of Literary Anecdotes* (Oxford: Oxford University Press, 1975)